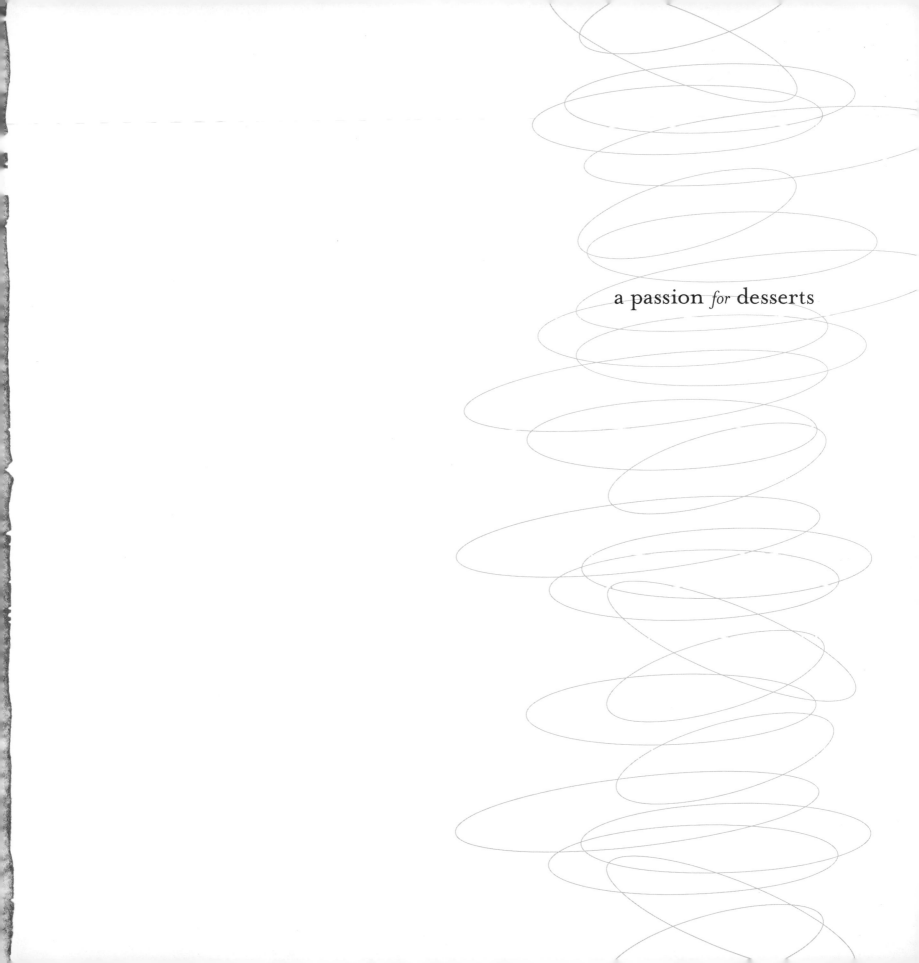

a passion *for* desserts

a passion *for* desserts

BY EMILY LUCHETTI

PHOTOGRAPHS BY MINH + WASS

CHRONICLE BOOKS
SAN FRANCISCO

Text copyright © 2003 by Emily Luchetti.
Photographs copyright © 2003 by Minh + Wass.
All rights reserved. No part of this book may
be reproduced in any form without written
permission from the publisher.

Library of Congress Cataloging-in-Publication
Data available.

ISBN 0-8118-3178-7

Manufactured in China.

Designed by Sara Schneider
Prop styling by Ngoc Minh Ngo
Food styling by Susie Theodorou

The photographers wish to thank
Emily Luchetti for her inspiring recipes
and Susie Theodorou for her unstinting
patience and humor on the set.
Special thanks to Keith, Jean, and most of all Lily.

Distributed in Canada by Raincoast Books
9050 Shaughnessy Street
Vancouver, British Columbia V6P 6E5

10 9 8 7 6 5 4 3 2 1

Chronicle Books LLC
85 Second Street
San Francisco, California 94105

www.chroniclebooks.com

TO PETER
FOR BETTER OR WORSE, HE'S NEVER TURNED DOWN A DESSERT

CONTENTS

PREFACE
9

INTRODUCTION
10

DESSERT BASICS
12

SPRING DESSERTS
30

SUMMER DESSERTS
64

AUTUMN DESSERTS
96

WINTER DESSERTS
132

FREQUENTLY USED RECIPES
166

RESOURCES
182

BIBLIOGRAPHY
185

ACKNOWLEDGMENTS
186

INDEX
187

TABLE OF EQUIVALENTS
192

preface

I come from a family of food lovers. My grandmother won the 1964 National Sunbeam Chicken Cooking Contest for her Blushing Chicken recipe. (She got a tableful of electric appliances and a red velvet cape and crown.) My grandfather either clipped or hand copied (this was before copy machines) hundreds of recipes. Many of these he cooked, but the majority made up a collection that he planned to cook "someday." I still have a shoe box full of these little bits of paper. My dad saved margarine tubs for the homemade pâté he gave to neighbors at Christmastime.

The first recipe I wrote (at age six) was for a mayonnaise sandwich: 2 pieces of white bread (preferably Pepperidge Farm) with Hellmann's Mayonnaise in between. My family thought it quite disgusting (and still tease me about it to this day), but little did any of us realize at the time where that first creative endeavor would lead me. In the mid-1970s and 1980s, my parents owned a cookware shop on Sanibel Island, Florida, called The Unpressured Cooker. I worked summers there during college, stocking every nook and cranny with feather pastry brushes, egg timers, Junior League cookbooks from all fifty states, food processors, woks, and chef's knives.

After college I embarked on a culinary career that began on the savory side of the kitchen. In 1987 I switched to desserts and now, after more than fifteen years as a pastry chef, teacher, and author of two dessert cookbooks, I find it impossible not to spend at least some portion of my day thinking about, preparing, or eating something sweet. Asking me not to bake is like asking a salmon not to swim. Over the years, my infatuation with pastry has taken three forms: capturing the essence of the seasons, understanding ingredients, and entertaining, and it is these I hope to share in this book.

While we appreciate the nuances of savory food, it does not invoke the same pleasure we get from eating desserts. Sighs of satisfaction are much louder over Raspberry Ice Cream Sandwiches (page 151) or Bittersweet Chocolate Mousse Cake with White Chocolate Sauce (page 139) than a salmon fillet with tomato basil sauce, no matter how exquisite. It is the ability to bring this simple joy to both my family and complete strangers that continually drives me into the kitchen. But I do not want to stop there—I want to pass on this enthusiasm. I want you to go into your kitchen, take the sugar and flour out of your cupboard, open this cookbook, and find the same pleasure in making desserts as I do. I want to make you, too, a passionate baker.

introduction

The recipes in this book are organized around the seasons of the year, each with its special fruits and flavors to use in creating desserts: Baked Pears with Almond Streusel (page 35) in spring, Berry Crème Fraîche Cake (page 69) for summer, Apple Splits (page 102) in fall, Hot Buttered Rum and Banana Compote (page 138) in winter. With such desserts we translate a season into a dish, starting with going to the market and finding strawberries in blossoming spring, cherries in summer heat, apples as the leaves begin to turn, and bright orange tangerines when it is cold. Appreciate what each season has to offer and use it to its maximum potential.

Wherever you live, something is grown locally. Find it, learn about it, and use it. Cooking with local foods will increase the taste of your desserts immensely. And be aware that the first fruits of a season are not always the best. Hold out for a couple of weeks, and the strawberries will be sweeter and the apples crisper. At the end of the season, say farewell and patiently wait for next year, when the bounty will reappear.

Even ingredients that are available year-round, such as chocolate and nuts, make different contributions to desserts from one season to the next. In the winter they are used with a heavier hand than in summer, when flavors are light. When it is cold, Coffee Chocolate Towers (page 44) are popular, while hot weather draws us to Chocolate Chip Ice Cream Cake (page 78). Many desserts in this book can be made in more than one season: use the seasonal breakdown as a guide, not a strict rule.

To gain skill as a baker, you must get to know ingredients and how to maximize their flavors. Bittersweet chocolate will produce a different result than semisweet chocolate. Very ripe fruit will not bake or taste the same as slightly underripe fruit. Sugar is crucial in making pastry, but too much will detract from the natural flavor of the main ingredient. The first taste of a great dessert should be of the primary ingredient—whether pecans, chocolate, or raspberries—not of sugar.

In designing a dessert, pastry chefs test many versions of it until they get the proper balance of all the components. It can be a lengthy process. Two clues let me know when I am finished creating a dessert: One is when I can't help but take another bite immediately after the first. The second is when I wake up in the middle of the night, think about the dessert, and am able to go back to sleep and not twist and turn, trying to figure out what it is missing.

Another element of making a dessert or using a given ingredient lies in being familiar with its history. Knowing the lineage of a Meyer lemon as I pick it off a tree to use in a Meyer Lemon Buttermilk Tart (page 160), learning that in the 1800s chocolate was drunk as a digestive by European upperclass women, and understanding how Peach Melba (page 95) got its name—such information can increase our appreciation of desserts and place their ingredients in a larger context.

For me, though, the keenest satisfaction is simply in seeing a group of people laughing and lingering around the table as they enjoy a fresh tart or pudding that I made—this is truly the most rewarding moment of a baker's day. It used to be that if you really wanted to impress people, you took them to a fancy restaurant. Now the reverse is true. It is much more hospitable to bring guests into your home.

Today's media offers a constant, almost intimidating, flow of information on cooking, baking, and entertaining. Television programs, magazines, books, newspapers, classes, and the Internet show us what to do, when to do it, how to do it, and even where to do it. But entertaining at home is not about making a croquembouche for forty or creating a spun-sugar sculpture. It is about offering a festive, relaxing experience through good food and good company. By itself, an individual party or gathering may not seem significant, but over a lifetime, you will create many memorable occasions and add a richness to your life and others'. I hope the dessert recipes in this cookbook will help you do just that.

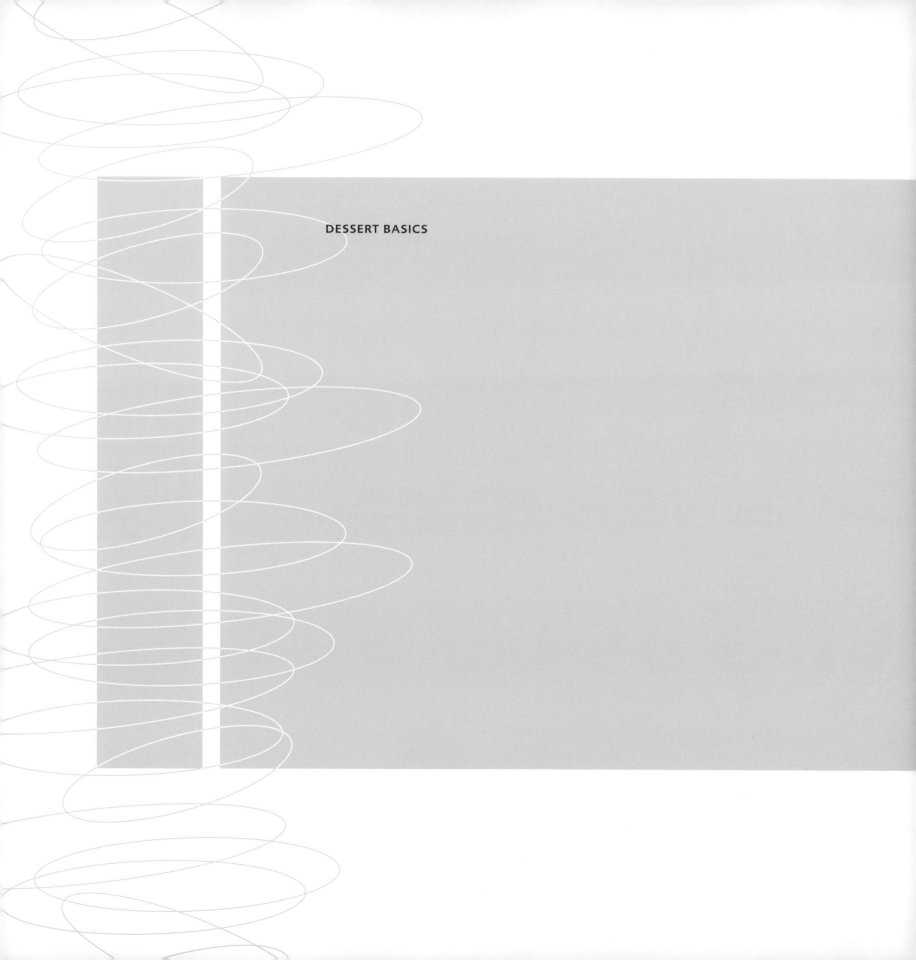

DESSERT BASICS

14 equipment

22 ingredients

28 tips and techniques

dessert basics

EQUIPMENT

You don't necessarily need a great deal of specialized equipment to enjoy baking and creating superb-tasting desserts. If you like to cook, however, you probably derive a large amount of pleasure in browsing for, discovering, and purchasing new utensils. For such people, there is always room for one more gadget in the kitchen! Fortunately for your cupboard space, many of the items used in making desserts serve double duty in savory cooking. | I have broken down this equipment list into three categories, for three levels of bakers: Getting Started, Committed, and Happily Over the Top. These are not determined by skill level but by the amount of baking you do. Remember, one person's luxury is another person's necessity, so peruse the lists and get whatever makes you a happier and better baker. See Resources (page 182) for recommended stores, catalogs, and Web sites.

getting started

BAKING PANS: Good-quality bakeware does not have to be expensive. I like heavy-duty aluminum pans. Nonstick can be an advantage in some recipes, but if regular pans are properly prepared, you can get by without them. You will need the following sizes:

> One 9-inch square pan with 2-inch sides
> Two or three 9-inch round cake pans
> One 9-by-13-inch pan with 2-inch sides
> Two baking sheets, 14 to 18 inches long and 12 to 13 inches wide
> One 9-inch pie pan
> One 9-inch tart pan with removable bottom
> One muffin pan with 12 muffin wells, each about $1/3$ cup
> One 9- or 10-inch Bundt pan

BOWLS: Assortment of various sizes, preferably stainless steel. These are practical for multiple uses. I like stainless steel because they are inexpensive, lightweight, and unbreakable and can cool down mixtures quickly. Get bowls with a wide shape to make mixing easy and efficient.

COOKBOOKS: Cookbooks are like T-shirts—you can always have one more. I buy some for the photographs, some for the general information, and some for the recipes.

ELECTRIC MIXER, HANDHELD: You can mix desserts by hand, but with a small investment you can make the work a lot easier, quicker, and more fun, with better results. Be sure your mixer has a heavy-duty motor, and beater and whip attachments are nice to have, too. KitchenAid mixers work very well. When using a handheld mixer, it is very important to scrape down the sides of the bowl and make sure the ingredients mix uniformly. I hold the mixer in one hand and a spatula in the other, and push the mixture toward the beater. Depending on the type of mixer you have, mixing times can vary considerably. When following recipes, look for appearance rather than time as a guide.

ICE CREAM SCOOP: Large spoons can do the job, but scoops create a classic round shape. I prefer scoops with spring-loaded release latches as the ice cream falls from the scoop easier. Dip the scoop in water after every couple of scoops to keep the ice cream from sticking.

KNIVES: It is important to choose knives that feel comfortable in your hand. Good-quality knifes will last a lifetime. Do not put them in the dishwasher—it will dull the blades. For baking you can get by with just three: a paring knife, a 10- or 12-inch chef's knife, and a serrated knife.

MEASURING CUPS AND SPOONS: Either plastic or metal will do for spoons and dry ingredient cups. Get two sets of spoons and use one for liquid ingredients and one for dry. This way you don't have to dry them between measurements. Measure dry ingredients in specific-sized cups ($1/4$ cup, $1/2$ cup, etc.) for the most accuracy. Measure liquids in a clear glass container. Pyrex with its bright lettering is easy to read. I have the 1-, 2-, and 8-cup sizes. I also like The Perfect Beaker, a measuring cup in the shape of a beaker, with different measurements all around it.

METAL RULER: Use for measuring the width and thickness of doughs. The metal makes it easy to keep clean.

METAL SIEVE (MEDIUM): One from the savory side of your kitchen will work fine.

OVEN THERMOMETER: Taylor is a good brand. Keep it in your oven and check it each time you use your oven.

PARCHMENT PAPER: I could wax poetic about parchment paper (which is ironic, since one of its pluses over wax paper is that it doesn't have any wax in it!). I use parchment paper constantly. In most cases, there is no need to grease pans—just use parchment paper. Sift dry ingredients onto a piece of parchment, then add them to the batter by picking up the paper, forming a chute, and pouring them in. This is much neater than trying to add them from a bowl. Line a baking sheet with it when making cookies: When the cookies are done, remove the tray of cookies from the oven and simply slide the parchment paper (and the cookies) onto a countertop or rack. Cool the baking sheet slightly and then bake another batch. Some stores sell parchment next to aluminum foil and plastic wrap, some in the baking aisle. Get flat sheets of parchment paper at a kitchen or restaurant supply store, if you prefer not to deal with those pesky rolls.

PASTRY BLENDER: A set of rows of wire whips with a handle on top, this is great for making crusts. It breaks the butter up into the flour without overmixing or making the butter soft. It is just as good, if not better, than more expensive alternatives.

PASTRY BRUSH: Dedicate a brush just for making pastry. You don't want your pastries tasting like garlic. Brushes retain odors even when run through the dishwasher.

POT HOLDERS: Get the kind made from heavy-duty terry cloth. These are obligatory in my kitchen. They are thick enough so the heat from a pan won't pass through the cloth before you set it down and they can be washed repeatedly with little shrinkage.

RUBBER SPATULAS, HEAT-RESISTANT: Anyone who has worn down and/or melted the end of a plastic spatula will appreciate the new heat-resistant choices. They won't fall apart when used in hot liquids or after repeated use. They come in bright colors that not only let you coordinate them to your kitchen but also make finding them in a drawer or utensil holder a snap.

TIMER: Electronic, manual, or artichoke shaped, it's a matter of personal preference. Just make sure it has a loud and long enough ringer that you will hear it.

VEGETABLE PEELER: There are many styles of vegetable peelers, but as with knives and whisks, get what feels good in your hand. I like the Swiss vegetable peelers. They are shaped like a Y—the crosspiece is the blade. They are light and remove a vegetable's or fruit's skin without taking much flesh.

WHISKS: Purchase whisks that have flexible wires, making mixing easier on your wrist and arm. The length of handles varies; use whichever feels the most comfortable in your hand. At a minimum get a medium-size whisk, about 8 inches long (without the handle). Add different sizes as you need them.

committed

Include all items in the Getting Started category, plus the following.

ANGEL FOOD CAKE PAN: This is a specialty item, as it cannot be used for many things besides angel food cake. But try to make an angel food cake in another type of pan, and it won't come out as light.

BAKING DISHES, CERAMIC: Available in many shapes and sizes. Desserts like bread pudding, crisps, cobblers, and baked pears can be baked and served in the same container.

BAKING SHEET WITH 1-INCH SIDES (JELLY-ROLL PAN): These I use as cookie sheets and for thin cakes. Great on the savory side for vegetables and meats.

BLOWTORCH: If you want to make crème brûlée, one of these is essential. Choose between the small retail blowtorch sold at cookware stores and the larger commercial kind found at hardware stores. Alternative methods, such as putting custards under the broiler, don't do brûlées justice. Blowtorches are also good for Baked Alaska.

BOWLS, ALL-CLAD STAINLESS-STEEL: These beautiful bowls with a lip to use as a handle come in various sizes.

COOKIE CUTTERS: Beyond the traditional Christmas or Hanukkah cookie cutters, there is an endless array to choose from. Don't show restraint in collecting them—they don't take up much room in your kitchen drawers and they are cheap. See Resources (page 182) for Web sites with hundreds of choices.

CORER: Use to quickly and cleanly remove the core from an apple or pear.

CRÊPE PAN: I use a thin metal pan designed especially for crêpes and a nonstick pan, both about 6 inches in diameter. Both work well. The crêpes from the metal pan have more color and are a little thinner, but you don't have to worry about seasoning nonstick pans.

FOOD PROCESSOR: For grinding nuts, processing fruit, and making some doughs.

ICE CREAM MACHINE: Machines with Freon inserts (by Cuisinart and Krups) make nicely textured ice cream. Their only drawback is the need to freeze the insert overnight before making ice cream. Other ice cream makers, such as those by White Mountain, require layering ice and rock salt around the machine during freezing. It's a bit of an effort, but they produce good-quality results. You can still buy hand-crank machines if you want to work for your ice cream.

JUICE REAMER: A hand gadget that lets you get more juice out of a lemon than just by squeezing it. The OXO reamer, with its black handle and polished cast-aluminum end, is sleek looking and fits well in the hand.

LOAF PANS: The traditional loaf pan is 5 inches wide, but I also like ones that are 3 to 4 inches wide. They allow you to cut thicker slices that look better on a dessert plate. Keep in mind that if you use a smaller loaf pan than the one specified in a recipe, you might have extra batter or mousse.

MELON BALLER: Can be used to make round shapes of many fruits, like apples and pears, not just melons. Also good for scooping truffles.

MICROPLANE GRATER: The perfect tool to remove peel from citrus. No more scraped knuckles from box scrapers or having to pick the peel out of grater holes. A good amount of peel gets stuck in box scrapers, affecting the yield. Traditional zesters work well, but you have to zest and chop. With a microplane grater, a couple of passes and you are done.

PASTRY, OR BENCH, SCRAPER: This is used to cut butter into flour for puff pastry or pie and tart doughs. It is also great for scraping dough pieces from a countertop. Get a metal one.

PIPING BAGS: My preference is disposable, as pastry bags are a pain to clean. After I use the nondisposable ones, I turn them inside out and run them through the dishwasher on the top rack. A self-sealing plastic bag can be substituted as a piping bag. You won't get quite the same control, but it will work in a pinch. Fill, seal, and cut off one of the corners.

PIPING TIPS: One star and one plain tip, each about $1/4$ to $1/2$ inch.

RAMEKINS, INDIVIDUAL CERAMIC: A set of eight 4-ounce ramekins is great to have around. They can be used not only for soufflés but also for custards, individual cakes, and any recipe that calls for an individual ovenproof dish. On the nonpastry side of the kitchen, they can be used to hold nuts, condiments, dipping sauces, or olives.

ROLLING PINS: There are two kinds of rolling pins: traditional with handles, and French, which come either tapered at the ends or completely straight. Both work well; selection is up to your personal preference. When you are at the kitchenware store, "test drive" both kinds and purchase whichever feels more comfortable.

SAUTÉ PANS AND SAUCEPANS: Choose heavy-bottomed pans. They cook more uniformly and keep custards from burning. You will find yourself using them daily for savory cooking as well. Two sauté pans (9 and 12 inches) and five saucepans (2 cups, 1, 2, 4, and 6 quarts) will cover your baking needs.

SCALE (SMALL): Weigh chocolate and nuts for more accurate baking. A small scale is not expensive.

SILICON BAKING SHEETS: Reusable silicone mats that can be used to line baking sheets. Good for spreading out caramel. Just wash with warm soapy water.

SLOTTED SPOONS: These are great for removing fruit from liquid either in a bowl or pan.

SPRINGFORM PANS: These pans are traditionally used for cheesecakes but can be used for all cakes. I like the 9-inch size, as 10-inch pans make too long a slice.

STAND MIXER: I have a 5-quart KitchenAid stand mixer and wouldn't want to bake without it. I encourage everyone who bakes to get one. It makes baking more fun and efficient, and you will be pleased with the results. Stand mixers are relatively expensive but last a long time. I still have the one I purchased in 1979.

SUGAR SHAKERS: Also called *dredgers*, they are used to dust powdered sugar or cocoa powder on top of desserts.

TART PANS, INDIVIDUAL: Get 4-inch pans with removable bottoms. Preparing individual tarts makes for a much grander presentation.

WOODEN SPATULAS, FLAT-ENDED: I use one of these when making custards. The flat edge makes sure nothing sticks to the bottom of the pan. It is also easier to see whether custard has thickened (by checking if it coats the spoon or spatula) with wood than plastic.

happily over the top

Include all items in the Getting Started and Committed categories, plus the following.

APPLE PEELER AND CORER: These contraptions clamp onto your countertop. One continuous hand crank cores, peels, and slices the apple. A must for anyone who is fond of apple desserts.

BABA AND SAVARIN MOLDS: Specialty molds are necessary for making these classic desserts. They can also be used for cakes and gelatin-based desserts.

BOWL FOR STAND MIXER: If you have a stand mixer and bake frequently, you will often come across recipes that require two different ingredients or sets of ingredients that need to be mixed separately. An extra work bowl saves you from transferring the mixture to another bowl and then cleaning the mixer bowl before you mix the second set of ingredients. For the same reason, get an extra whip.

BOWL FOR STAND MIXER, COPPER: Egg whites whip up thicker and higher in copper. KitchenAid makes a copper bowl especially for its mixer. With it, you get the advantage of copper and can watch it work, hands free.

CAKE COMB: Available in various sizes, cake combs are a simple way to get an attractive design on a cake.

CAKE TURNTABLE: Having the ability to put a cake on a revolving pedestal makes a cake easier to decorate, and the finished product will be more even.

CANDY THERMOMETER: One of these is good to have when making caramels or brittle. Get one that clips on to the side of the pan so you don't have to hold it over the boiling liquid.

CHERRY PITTER, HOPPER-STYLE: If you pit a substantial number of cherries, as I do, this is the pitter for you. With a feed funnel and spring-loaded steel plunger, it can pit cherries in rapid succession. It does tear them up a little more than if you pit each one separately, but if they are baked in a pie, no one will know the difference.

CHOCOLATE DIPPING FORKS: You can use a table fork when dipping chocolates, but these leave a thinner coating.

COOLING RACKS: Racks that fit your sheet pans are good for placing on top of puff pastry when it is baking to create mille-feuille. For glazing cakes: Lay parchment paper over a pan, then put a rack with the cake on top. Any glaze that lands on the parchment paper can be scooped up and put on the cake or saved for another use.

CROQUEMBOUCHE FORM: You can buy Styrofoam croquembouche forms that you cover with foil before assembling, but if you are going to go all out and make a croquembouche, get a stainless steel mold. It will look better as everyone takes off the profiteroles and dismantles it.

DOUGH CUTTER SETS: Cutters to cut dough come in all shapes: round, fluted, star, oval, square, and so on. Having a set makes sure you always have the proper size. Plus, they store very neatly in kitchen drawers.

ELECTRIC JUICER: You'll want one of these for recipes that call for a lot of juice. Can also be used for orange juice for breakfast.

FLEXIPANS: These come in many interesting shapes. They can be used for baked cakes, mousse desserts with gelatin, and frozen desserts. I do not use them when I want a nice brown crust, though. Metal does a better job, as it is a better conductor of heat.

GINGER GRATER: These flat metal or ceramic graters are better for grating ginger than box scrapers, which keep most of the ginger stuck in the grater holes.

ICE CREAM BOMBE MOLDS: These are very special and can be found in specialty cookware stores and flea markets. I display mine in the kitchen between uses to show them off.

ICE CREAM MACHINE WITH BUILT-IN FREON UNIT: If you want to make different flavors or even a good amount of the same kind of ice cream and get impatient waiting for a separate Freon unit to freeze, then one of these machines is for you. You can continuously make ice cream and sorbets until you run out of ingredients or freezer space, whichever comes first.

ICE CREAM SCOOPS (SMALL): Ice cream scoops that hold 2 teaspoons (about 1 inch across) and 2 tablespoons (about 1³/4 inches across) are great for scooping ice cream, forming cookies, and making truffles.

ICE CREAM SPADE: Used to scrape down the sides of an ice cream container, these can also be used to serve ice cream when, for appearance, you want a chunk of ice cream rather than the traditional scoop.

LADLES: Used more on the savory side of the kitchen than the sweet, small ladles (1 to 2 ounces) place sauces on plates very neatly. I use them when plating desserts at the restaurant.

MADELEINE MOLDS: Madeleine batter can be made in advance and refrigerated. With a madeleine pan on hand, at a moment's notice you can bake (and serve warm) some of these delectable cakelike cookies. Sure beats the packaged kind.

PASTRY WHEEL, FLUTED: For attractive lattice pie borders or edges on rolled cookies, these are fast and accurate.

PASTRY DOCKER: Used to make holes over the top of puff pastry to create millefeuille, a pastry docker is a real time-saver. A fork works, but as you are making the seemingly endless holes with just one fork, you will have time to think about how nice it would be to have a docker that gets the job done in no time flat.

PIPING TIPS: I use the star and plain tips the most, so I have a set of each in graduated sizes.

POTS AND PANS: All-Clad or KitchenAid in stainless steel, or Le Creuset in cast iron covered with enamel. These pots are worth the splurge. You will use them in your daily savory cooking. Le Creuset pots are heavy, but they keep your arms in shape!

SCALE, BALANCE OR DIGITAL: Balance (old-fashioned) and digital (high-tech) scales are accurate and easy to use. Invest in one, and your baking will be more precise.

ROTARY BEATER: Whipping 1 or 2 egg whites with an electric mixer can be a bit awkward. It's a small amount for a rather large piece of equipment. For small amounts of egg whites, I like using an old-fashioned rotary beater. It whips quickly and efficiently.

SIEVES, FINE AND MEDIUM-FINE MESH: Good-quality mesh strainers will last a long time. The fine mesh will strain out even raspberry seeds.

SPATULAS, OFFSET: Small offset spatulas with a 3-inch blade work well for smaller frosting jobs, like cupcakes or cookies. Larger ones with a 6-inch blade make spreading cake batter and frosting cakes less awkward. They are also nice for taking individual glazed cakes off of icing racks. A large metal hamburger spatula is not a pastry tool, but it is offset and useful for transferring cakes or tarts.

SPICE GRINDER: Grind cinnamon, ginger, and allspice just before you need them for optimal flavor. I like OXO brand grinders.

STEAMED PUDDING MOLDS: You can't make a good steamed pudding without one of these. (A cross between a pudding and a cake, steamed puddings are underappreciated today.) Found in cookware shops and flea markets, the molds are inexpensive, so pick one up.

STICK BLENDER, HANDHELD: The Braun stick blender is amazing to use for emulsifying a chocolate ganache or even a broken crème anglaise. It is easier to use than a blender, as the mixture can be left in the original pot or bowl.

TAMIS: Used for sifting, this is a much better tool than a traditional sifter or a sieve. Its wide, flat shape makes sifting efficient and fast.

TART SHELLS, MINI: For a dessert buffet or what we call "Small Endings" at Farallon, mini tart shells can be used for one-bite desserts. Fill with anything you would put in a large tart shell.

THERMOMETER: Once you get in the habit of using a thermometer, it will take most of the guesswork out of knowing when something is thick enough and make your baking more consistent. Get an instant-read thermometer with both Fahrenheit and Celsius.

TONGS: OXO makes great tongs. They are easy to grip, have good spring action, and stay together in the kitchen drawer. I use them for removing individual ramekins from water baths and dipping brioche in fruit puree to make summer puddings.

INGREDIENTS

Baking relies heavily on supermarket staples such as butter, sugar, flour, and eggs. Do not arbitrarily take what is on sale or most convenient from the grocery store shelf. Think a little bit about where your ingredients come from and what is in them. Good-quality ingredients are crucial for great-tasting desserts.

baking soda and baking powder

Check the expiration dates on the baking soda and baking powder in your cupboard. They are there for a reason. Both baking soda and baking powder help baked goods rise. To work properly, baking soda must have an acid included in the ingredients such as nonalkalized cocoa powder, lemon juice, buttermilk, or brown sugar. Baking powder is often called "double acting" since it works on two levels: one when the dry and wet ingredients are mixed, and again from the hot air of the oven.

butter

TYPES/QUALITY: I recommend unsalted butter for baking and cooking. It has a sweeter taste and lets you control the amount of salt you use. The quantity of salt varies in salted butter, and this can affect recipes. Wrap butter well in plastic wrap or in a self-sealing plastic bag since it absorbs odors easily. Always choose butter that is firm when cold. Softer butter has a higher moisture content. All butter must have a minimum of 80% fat. (The remaining 20% is water and milk solids.) It takes 10 quarts of milk to make 1 pound of butter. Throughout the year, butter can vary. The weather influences the quality of the grass a cow eats. Spring grass has a higher moisture content than winter grass, so the butter will have more moisture in it. The weather also affects the color of butter. In winter it is pale yellow and in summer it is a deep yellow. Natural food coloring is added to maintain a consistent color throughout the year. European-style butter has a higher butterfat content (82% to 86%), less moisture, and is often cultured. It has a richer, creamier taste. Brand names include Keller's (Plugra), Land O' Lakes, and Vermont Butter and Cheese.

MEASURING: Measure butter by weight. Sticks of butter vary in shape depending on the manufacturer. Some are short and fat, others long and narrow. They are all the same overall size. One stick is 4 ounces. Divide the stick in half for 2 ounces, and so on. The paper or foil wrapped around butter is conveniently marked for easy measuring. Measuring by tablespoons, especially when using large amounts, can be inaccurate.

SOFTENING: When a recipe calls for soft butter, it should be malleable, not so soft that it looks greasy. Let butter soften at room temperature. Using a microwave softens it unevenly. Whipped butter should not be used in baking.

STORING: Sweet butter can be frozen for up to 5 months and should be kept for no more than a couple of weeks in the refrigerator after the sell-by date.

chocolate

TYPES/QUALITY: Avoid chocolate that comes wrapped in 1-ounce packages—it doesn't have the subtleties or complexity that higher-quality brands have and is very thick when melted. Coating chocolate should also be avoided as it has a waxy taste. Some grocery stores place chocolate for baking in both the baking aisle and the candy aisle. Be sure to look in both places. In the candy aisle, read the labels to make sure you are not buying candy bars. See Resources (page 182) for chocolate sources.

DARK CHOCOLATE: I use bittersweet chocolate in all recipes that call for dark chocolate. It has much more flavor than semisweet. Some companies offer several different kinds of bittersweet chocolate. I like Callebaut, El Rey, Ghirardelli, Guittard, Lindt 70% Excellence, Michel Cluziel, Scharffen Berger, and Valrhona.

MILK CHOCOLATE: It should not be compared to dark chocolate in taste. When it is, milk chocolate is shortchanged, as it is not as intense in flavor. But it isn't trying to be dark chocolate. Milk and dark chocolates each have their own unique characteristics. When using milk chocolate, it is important to pick one of good quality. Many brands taste dull, as the addition of milk can dilute the intensity of the chocolate. El Rey from Venezuela makes my favorite milk chocolate. It has a rich deep taste, perfect for eating and baking. Valrhona is also an excellent choice.

WHITE CHOCOLATE: This is not really chocolate because it doesn't have any chocolate liquor in it, but it is delicious used in desserts, especially when paired with fruits. (Unlike many people, I am not a fan of pairing dark chocolate and fruits.) White chocolate brands I like include Callebaut, El Rey, and Valrhona.

MEASURING: Measure chocolate by weight rather than using a measuring cup. How the chocolate is cut can greatly affect the cup measurement.

MELTING: Finely chop the chocolate. Bring a pot one-third full of water to a boil. Turn off the heat and place a stainless-steel bowl over the water (you can also use a double boiler). Make sure the bowl is sitting over, not in, the water, as chocolate will scorch if it gets too hot. (To check this, place the bowl on the pot and then pick it up to see if there is any water on the bottom of the bowl.) The residual heat will melt the chocolate. While the chocolate is melting, stir occasionally. If you haven't stirred the chocolate while it was melting, it may look unmelted on top, but the rest of it could be melted. This is especially important with milk and white chocolates since they scorch easily.

STORING: Store chocolate away from heat and light. Wrap in foil once opened.

cocoa powder

Good-quality cocoa powder adds richness and color to desserts. While many stores carry high-quality chocolate, it is difficult to find good cocoa powder. I use Green and Black, Michel Cluziel Dark Red, and Valrhona cocoa powders. At the time this book is going to press, El Rey is developing a cocoa powder. See Resources (page 182) for online sources.

coconut

TYPE: I prefer unsweetened coconut in my desserts. There is already enough sugar in most recipes, and sweetened coconut is very sweet. Unsweetened coconut can be found in gourmet and health food stores.

TOASTING: Spread the coconut meat in a single layer on a baking sheet. Bake in a preheated 325 degree F oven for about 10 minutes, until golden brown. Stir occasionally for even browning. Keep a sharp eye on it while it is in the oven. Coconut burns very quickly.

coffee

If I am making a coffee dessert, I will crush coffee beans and infuse them in the liquid. This gives a delicious rich coffee flavor. If I add it in powdered form, I prefer Medaglia D'Oro instant espresso. It dissolves quickly and gives an intense flavor. As with wine, never use coffee that you wouldn't want to drink in desserts.

cooking oil spray

I use vegetable-oil cooking spray to grease pans. It is quicker to spray than to spread butter with a pastry brush. Be sure to use nonhydrogenated oil with a neutral taste and no artificial flavors.

dairy

CREAM: Cream nomenclature can be confusing. Some companies have more than one kind, each with different amounts of fat and different names. Buy heavy whipping cream, sometimes simply called heavy cream. Cream labeled whipping cream (without the word heavy) is a little lower in fat. While it will work in recipes, it isn't quite as creamy. Avoid light cream. Check the labels—you want the cream with the highest amount of fat. Do not buy ultrapasteurized cream. It has a longer shelf life but when whipped, does not increase as much in volume. It also does not taste as fresh, does not hold its whip as long, and goes from underwhipped to overwhipped very quickly. If your local supermarket sells only ultrapasteurized cream, look for your cream in a health food store.

CRÈME FRAÎCHE: Crème fraîche is a beautiful alternative to Chantilly cream. It tastes cool and creamy like sour cream but has a more subtle, sophisticated, and somewhat nutty flavor. It can be served sweetened or unsweetened, whichever you prefer. Depending on what flavors it is being paired with, I serve it both ways. Long a staple of French cuisine, crème fraîche has been available in U.S. grocery stores and cheese shops only in the last several years. It is available in both European and American brands. Taste and texture fluctuate between brands, so try several. It can be rather expensive. You can easily make your own (see page 172) but it does take at least 48 hours to thicken. So do what I do: buy it if you need to use it right away and make it when you can allocate enough time.

MILK: Whole milk should be used in baking. Save skim, 1%, or 2% milk for your cereal.

eggs

SIZE/FRESHNESS: I use large eggs in all my recipes. Buy eggs at a store that has a high turnover so you know they are fresh. The labeling of egg expiration dates written on cartons varies from company to company. Some place sell-by or use-by dates and/or numerical codes on the ends of cartons. Many code by listing the number of the day in the year the egg was laid, followed by the last number in the year. For example, if an egg was laid on January 15, 2003, the carton would read 153.

TIPS: Keep eggs refrigerated and if using them in a cake or cookie recipe, bring them to room temperature by letting them sit on the countertop for 15 to 30 minutes.

If you separate eggs in advance, cover the bowl of yolks with plastic wrap to prevent a skin from forming.

Egg whites whipped without sugar are easier to overwhip than those that have sugar added. In either case, watch them closely.

filo

Most filo in your grocer's freezer section comes under the names Athens, which comes in a yellow box, and Apollo, which comes in a white box. The same company makes both. Apollo filo is slightly thicker and will have a flat look to it after it is baked. Athens filo is thinner and has a shiny appearance. I prefer the Athens brand and have based my recipes on it. If Apollo is all you can find, it will work fine—just be aware that the sheet dimensions are not quite the same. Be sure to allow time for the filo to defrost in the refrigerator before using.

flour

I primarily use unbleached all-purpose flour in baking. Gold Medal, Pillsbury, and King Arthur make a consistent quality product. Cake flour produces a cake with a very fine crumb. In cakes where I want a more delicate yet not too crumbly texture, I will use half cake flour and half all-purpose flour. My friend and pastry teacher, Carolyn Weil, gave me the idea of keeping a chopstick in my flour container. Stir the flour before measuring to aerate it slightly.

lemon Juice

Although the lemon-shaped plastic bottle of lemon juice is extremely convenient, it is better to squeeze juice from fresh lemons. The flavor is more lemony and fresher. Taste the two side-by-side and you will notice the difference. This also is true if you compare two-day-old lemon juice and just-squeezed lemon juice. The latter is far superior.

nuts

Nuts are a great addition to desserts. They can be used as the primary ingredient or as a garnish.

TIPS: Nut substitutions can be made for most of the recipes in this book, so use whichever is your favorite.

I prefer to weigh nuts for a recipe rather than use a measuring cup. This is especially important if the nuts are whole. Measurements fluctuate depending on how tightly the nuts are packed.

Natural almonds, those with the skin on, give more flavor to desserts. Many recipes call for blanched nuts to create a neutral-color dessert. I favor both the added color and the added taste of the natural nut.

TOASTING: Put them in a single layer on a baking sheet. Bake in a preheated 300 degree F oven until lightly colored, about 20 minutes. The lower temperature colors the nuts more evenly without burning them and brings out their flavor. I have never understood why people toast nuts in a skillet on top of the stove. It is much too labor-intensive. You must make sure each of the nuts is turned over so it cooks evenly on both sides. Putting them in the oven is much simpler. Nuts with a higher oil content like macadamia nuts color more quickly than nuts like almonds, which have a lower amount of fat. Macadamia nuts can often only be found salted. In this case, rinse them off in a strainer under running water. Dry them in a towel and then toast them. This works with other nuts, too. Don't grind toasted nuts while they are still warm. The heat will turn them into paste.

SKINNING HAZELNUTS: This job can be rather tedious. I use a fryer basket or colander. The rough texture of the basket loosens the skins, and the holes are big enough for the skins to fall through. Don't worry about getting the nuts completely clean— you just want to remove any flaky pieces. You can drive yourself nuts (!) trying to get off every last piece.

spices

Bakers often buy spices and leave them in the back of their kitchen cupboards for a long time before they are used up. The good news about this practice is that spices should be stored in the dark since sunlight dissipates their intensity. The bad news is that age affects them, too, so they should be used up within several months of the purchase date. Purchase the smallest container available. Buy from a company that sells a lot of spices, ensuring constant rotation of product. See the listing for Penzey's, a high-quality spice company, in Resources (page 182).

sugar

BRANDS: What would a baker do without sugar? I buy 10-pound bags to make sure I never run out. On the west coast of the United States, I use C&H, and on the east coast, Dominos. They are both made of pure cane as opposed to beets.

BROWN SUGAR: I prefer dark brown sugar to light brown sugar as it has a more intense molasses flavor. Either dark or light can be used in these recipes.

CONFECTIONERS' SUGAR: This is powdered granulated sugar. It has cornstarch added to it to prevent it from lumping.

SUPERFINE SUGAR: Many bakers use superfine sugar, which is simply granulated sugar that is more finely ground. C&H recently introduced a superfine sugar. You can also make it by processing granulated sugar in a food processor. Superfine sugar is sometimes preferred in cakes as it dissolves more quickly. The recipes in this book will work with either superfine or regular granulated sugar.

vanilla

PRODUCTION: Vanilla beans are extremely labor-intensive to produce. The blossom of each flower (a member of the orchid family) opens only one day per year and must be hand pollinated. After the hard green pods are harvested, they are briefly boiled and placed in the sun to dry. At night they are wrapped in blankets so they can sweat. This heating and sweating process is repeated for several months until the beans shrink substantially and take on their familiar dark brown color. Vanilla is primarily produced in Madagascar, Mexico, and Tahiti.

FORMS: Once the pods are harvested, they are sold as either whole beans or processed further and sold as extract, bean paste, or vanilla powder. I have used vanilla in all these forms in my recipes. They all work. Many recipes call for infusing a vanilla pod in cream or milk. Once this is done, there is still a lot of flavor left in the bean. Rinse it off and dry it in a very low oven or at room temperature. Once dry, put in a closed container of sugar for several days. You will end up with fragrant vanilla sugar that can be used in all your recipes. You can also finely grind the dried beans in a spice grinder and use them as powder.

BRANDS: The Nielsen Massey Company outside of Chicago (see Resources, page 182) sells wonderful vanilla pods, extracts, paste, and powder from Madagascar (also called Bourbon), and Mexican and Tahitian beans. Flavor Organics is another good-quality extract. Never use imitation vanilla. It is better to omit vanilla altogether if you cannot get the real stuff.

timing and organization

The desserts in this book are sophisticated and full of flavor, yet simple to make. They have been created with the understanding that most of us must juggle dessert preparation around picking up the kids, getting out of work late, and cooking the rest of the menu. The trick is to know what things can be prepared in advance without sacrificing flavor and what should be made closer to serving time. For example, tart or pie shells can be made in advance and frozen but taste best baked the day they are to be consumed. Most sauces can be made in advance and warmed just before serving. Each recipe in this book contains tips that will allow you to organize dessert preparation around your own schedule.

ice baths

Ice baths are helpful to quickly cool down sauces and mousse mixtures. Fill a large bowl half full of ice. Add enough cold water to cover the ice. Nest the bowl of whatever you are cooling on top. Stir the mixture occasionally for even cooling.

making caramel

When making caramel, after the sugar water comes to a boil, brush the inside of the pan above the water line with a pastry brush dipped in water or cover the pan with a lid for 15 seconds. This will clean off any residual sugar.

It can be a tough job to clean a pan that has hard caramel stuck on the inside. Put some water in the pan and bring it to a boil. The hard pieces of caramel will melt when the water gets hot, and cleaning will be a breeze.

the dessert doctor

Let's face it, sometimes desserts don't come out exactly like we planned. Here are some tricks that will keep guests content and even unaware that something is amiss:

Serve the dessert in a bowl and call it a pudding.

Put a big dollop of Chantilly Cream on top.

Serve more wine before dessert is served.

Turn the lights down.

Serve with a flourish!

caring for strawberries

After you bring strawberries home from the market, take them out of the basket and place in a single layer on a tray lined with a paper towel. Leaving the strawberries in their container causes them to deteriorate much more quickly, and one bad berry will contaminate the others. If you are enjoying the berries that day, leave them on the counter. Refrigerate strawberries overnight but let them sit at room temperature for 15 minutes before serving to take the chill off and release their flavor and fragrance.

To clean strawberries, fill a large bowl with cold water, place the berries in the water, and gently swish them around with your hands. This allows any dirt or sand to sink to the bottom of the bowl and doesn't bruise the fruit. Lift the berries from the bowl and place them on a towel. Don't hull or cut the berries before washing so they won't get waterlogged. Wash the strawberries within several hours of when you plan to eat them.

cutting apples and pears

To get uniform apple and pear slices, place the fruit upright on a cutting board. Cut down on all 4 sides, three-quarters of the way toward the center, leaving just the core in the center. Lay the fruit pieces cut-side down and slice into the desired size.

mixing ingredients

When mixing ingredients together in a bowl, always choose a bowl a little bit larger as opposed to one on the small side. Mixing will be more efficient and smooth if you are not worried the mixture is going to overflow.

When using an electric mixer, stop the machine and scrape down the sides of the bowl. This will ensure even mixing of ingredients.

ice cream

Ice cream right out of the machine tastes incredible but is often too soft to scoop. It needs to set up, or "harden off," in the freezer. To quicken this process, I prefreeze my container for 30 minutes before I fill it with the newly churned ice cream. If your freezer freezes your ice cream so hard it is difficult to scoop, place the ice cream in the refrigerator for 10 to 15 minutes, then scoop it.

Ice cream always tastes wonderful, but should only be part of a dessert when needed to round out the flavor. With some desserts, adding ice cream may make the overall taste too intense.

measuring ingredients

Most cookbooks tell you to measure all your ingredients before beginning a recipe. There's a reason for this—it works! Your baking will be more accurate and you will have less of a tendency to omit something.

storing desserts

Use airtight containers for storing pavlovas, cookies, and meringues. Tin containers don't keep all the air out. Cakes and pies can be wrapped in a double layer of plastic wrap. Desserts with custard fillings should be refrigerated.

cutting cakes

For neatly cut cake pieces, use a hot dry knife. For each slice, dip a knife in hot water (or under a hot running faucet), wipe dry, and cut.

SPRING DESSERTS Spring offers the most dramatic changes within one season. It starts out cold and wet and closes warm and sunny. This is when we slowly venture from our winter cocoons. We don't take a spring day for granted when it has just been preceded by a harsh bitter wind. Perhaps the day is more beautiful for the wind that came before it. We know spring will come—it does every year—but each time we are relieved and ready when winter is finally over, flowers start to appear, and the weather begins to warm.

Spring brings us daylight saving time, strawberries, crocuses and daffodils, robins, shorts and white legs, Mother's Day, rhubarb, spring cleaning, the start of baseball season, maple syrup, rain showers, Saturday mornings at the garden nursery, snow in April, and Easter.

Deciding what to make for dessert is trickiest in this season. We must begin to lighten up desserts so that we are not completely dismayed when we pull our bathing suits from the back of the bottom drawer and tug them on. But this dessert shift cannot be done all at once, as the weather is schizophrenic. We start to crave lighter flavors, but the hanging on of the harsh weather draws us as well to hearty desserts. If cold winds are blowing, Rice Pudding Napoleon with Rum Raisins (page 32) is called for, but if the sun is warming your cheeks, Honey Cream–Strawberry Parfaits (page 46) should be on the menu. This is one season where you need to check the weather report before choosing your dessert.

32 rice pudding napoleon with rum raisins

35 baked pears with almond streusel

36 fifty-year apple cake

37 black mission fig honey cake

38 brown sugar meringues with strawberries

40 bourbon milk shake

41 frozen lemon parfait with lemon ginger
    and cassis sauces

43 caramel chocolate-chunk tart

44 coffee chocolate towers

46 honey cream–strawberry parfaits

47 milk chocolate cheesecake

48 ice wine ice cream with strawberry
    rhubarb compote

50 vanilla, caramel, and cinnamon-almond
    panna cottas

51 rhubarb orange tart

53 vanilla almond savarin with ginger
    ice cream balls

55 coconut pavlovas with lime curd, ginger
    ice cream, and papayas

56 passion fruit soufflés with mango sauce

59 strawberry ginger sodas with
    orange sherbet

61 walnut hazelnut bars

63 apple filo napoleons

Blitz Puff Pastry (page 168)

RICE PUDDING

1 teaspoon unsalted butter

$^1/_2$ cup Arborio rice

1 cup heavy (whipping) cream

2 $^1/_2$ cups milk

$^1/_2$ vanilla bean, split lengthwise and seeds removed

$^1/_3$ cup granulated sugar

RUM RAISINS

$^2/_3$ cup water

$^2/_3$ cup granulated sugar

$^1/_3$ cup dark rum

$^3/_4$ cup raisins

$^3/_4$ cup golden raisins

Confectioners' sugar, for dusting

rice pudding napoleon

WITH RUM RAISINS

Makes **8** servings

The most popular way to serve rum raisins is in ice cream. The sweet raisins, pungent rum, and smooth ice cream are a great combination. This dessert accomplishes the same goal but doesn't stop there: the rice pudding adds flavor along with creaminess, and the puff pastry contributes flakiness and crunch. In preparing the rum raisins, use both golden and dark raisins for extra color and select a dark rum like Myers's or Mount Gay for maximum flavor. Arborio rice is a better choice than other rice varieties, as each kernel can absorb more liquid and produce a creamier pudding. In an attempt to make a really creamy rice pudding, don't be tempted to use all cream. Milk is needed or the pudding will get too thick before the rice is cooked and will become a gluey mass resembling construction spackle. You can make all the components ahead of time but be sure to assemble them just before serving.

Line 2 baking sheets with parchment.

Cut the puff pastry into 2 pieces, 1 piece two-thirds of the dough, and the other one-third. Refrigerate or freeze the smaller piece and save it for another use. Lightly flour a work surface and the top of the larger piece of puff pastry. Roll the pastry out $^1/_8$ inch thick. Trim the edges to make a 16-by-15-inch rectangle. With a sharp knife or pizza cutter, cut the pastry into 20 pieces, each 4 by 3 inches. Lay the pieces 1 inch apart on the prepared baking sheets. Refrigerate for at least 1 hour to overnight.

Preheat the oven to 375 degrees F. Using a fork, make holes over the top of each piece of puff pastry. Place a second baking sheet or a wire rack on top of the pastry. (These steps will help create crisp, flaky layers.) Bake the puff pastry until very golden brown, 15 to 20 minutes. (If you have used a baking sheet on top of the pastry, you will have to remove it to check the color.)

TO MAKE THE RICE PUDDING: In a medium saucepan, melt the butter over medium heat. Stir in the rice and cook, stirring frequently to lightly toast it, about 1 minute. Add the cream, milk, and vanilla bean and bring the mixture to a boil over medium-high heat. Reduce the heat and simmer gently, stirring frequently, until the rice is tender, 20 to 25 minutes. Discard the vanilla bean. Stir in the granulated sugar. Transfer the rice pudding to a bowl and refrigerate until cold, at least 1 hour.

TO MAKE THE RUM RAISINS: Put the water, granulated sugar, and rum in a small saucepan. Bring to a boil and boil for 3 minutes. Stir in the raisins and continue to boil until the raisins are soft and the liquid is slightly syrupy, about 5 minutes. Transfer to a bowl and refrigerate until cold, about 30 minutes.

TO SERVE: Place a piece of puff pastry on each of 8 dessert plates. There will be extra pieces of puff pastry. Spread some raisins over the pastry and cover with some rice pudding. Top with a second piece of pastry. Dust with confectioners' sugar. Serve immediately.

PLANNING AHEAD: The rice pudding and the rum raisins can be made a day ahead and kept refrigerated. The puff pastry should be baked the day you plan to serve the napoleon.

baked pears

WITH ALMOND STREUSEL

Makes **8** servings

One of the most memorable picnics I have experienced took place in a California almond orchard in the middle of spring. My cousin's and my blanket was spread out under a forest of fragrant trees bursting with white flowers. Like any successful picnic, it made us feel suspended in time. Almond trees offer so much pleasure I could be content with them even if they did not have nuts. But luckily they do.

ALMOND PRODUCTION

In the spring, beehives are trucked to almond orchards, where the bees busily fly from blossom to blossom, gathering nectar for their honey and pollinating the blossoms. By July, a green fuzzy coating encases the almonds. That covering then dries out and shrivels, revealing the almond in its shell. At picking time in midsummer to early fall, a machine, appropriately called a shaker, grabs the trunk of each tree and vigorously agitates it, causing the almonds to fall to the ground. The nuts are then scooped up by a huge vacuum cleaner called a pickup machine.

4 firm ripe pears

ALMOND STREUSEL
6 tablespoons granulated sugar
6 tablespoons firmly packed brown sugar
$1/8$ teaspoon salt
6 tablespoons all-purpose flour
3 ounces (6 tablespoons) cold unsalted butter, cut into 1-inch pieces
3 ounces (3/4 cup) natural whole almonds, toasted (see page 26)

CREAM
$1/4$ vanilla bean or $1/4$ teaspoon vanilla bean paste
$1^{1}/2$ cups heavy (whipping) cream
3 tablespoons granulated sugar

Preheat the oven to 350 degrees F.

Peel the pears. Core them from the bottom, leaving the pears whole. Place them in a single layer, standing up, in an ovenproof baking dish. (If the pears won't sit upright, slice a thin piece off the bottom of each one.)

In a food processor, process the granulated sugar, brown sugar, salt, and flour. Add the butter and almonds. Using the pulse switch, process until the mixture begins to come together.

Press some streusel all over each of the pears, completely covering them. Bake the pears until the streusel is golden brown in color, about 25 minutes.

While the pears are baking, prepare the cream: If you are using the vanilla bean, slice it in half lengthwise and scrape out the seeds. Reserve the bean for another use. Place the seeds or vanilla bean paste in a medium bowl with the cream and granulated sugar. Whip the cream until thickened but still pourable.

TO SERVE: Put some cream in the bottom of each of 8 bowls. If some streusel fell off the pears during baking, spoon it back on. Place a warm pear in the middle of each bowl and spoon any remaining streusel around the pears. Serve immediately.

PLANNING AHEAD: The streusel can be made a day in advance and kept refrigerated. The pears can be baked earlier in the day and reheated in a preheated 350 degree F oven for 10 minutes. The cream can be made a couple of hours in advance.

fifty-year apple cake

Makes **8 to 12** servings

2 medium apples (such as Granny Smith or Pippin)

2 large eggs

2 cups sugar

2 teaspoons ground cinnamon

$^{1}/_{2}$ cup oil

1 $^{3}/_{4}$ ounces ($^{1}/_{2}$ cup) chopped walnuts

2 cups sifted all-purpose flour

1 teaspoon salt

2 teaspoons baking soda

1 cup golden raisins

8 scoops Vanilla Bean Ice Cream (page 179) or Chantilly Cream (page 172)

My friend Mary Sue's grandmother, also named Mary, created this recipe. She has measured, mixed, and baked it the same way for more than fifty years—the sure sign of a timeless recipe. It has a cult following from Monterey to Santa Rosa, California. Children who devoured it are now moms making it for their kids. You will find it so wonderful and quick to make, you will put it in the front of your recipe box ready at a moment's notice. Serve with Chantilly Cream or ice cream. Either way is delicious. | This recipe actually serves more than eight, but I like to restrict it to that number for a party so that I have some left over to go with my coffee the next morning.

Preheat the oven to 350 degrees F. Grease the bottom of a 9-by-13-inch baking pan and line it with parchment paper.

Peel, quarter, and core the apples. Cut into $^{1}/_{2}$-inch pieces. There should be about 3 cups of apple pieces.

In a large bowl, lightly whisk the eggs. Using a rubber spatula, stir in the sugar, cinnamon, oil, walnuts, and apples.

In another bowl, or on a piece of parchment paper, sift together the flour, salt, and baking soda. Stir it into the apple mixture. Stir in the raisins. The batter will be thick.

Spread the batter into the prepared pan. Bake until a skewer inserted in the middle comes out clean, about 45 minutes.

Let cool completely at room temperature. Run a knife around the inside edge of the pan to loosen the edges of the cake. Place a cutting board on top of the pan and invert the cake and the board. Remove the pan and carefully peel off the parchment paper.

TO SERVE: Cut the cake into 12 pieces. Place right-side up. Serve with Vanilla Bean Ice Cream or Chantilly Cream.

PLANNING AHEAD: The apple cake can be made a day in advance; store well wrapped in plastic wrap at room temperature.

black mission fig honey cake

Makes about **10** servings

3 tablespoons unseasoned bread crumbs

8 ounces (16 tablespoons) unsalted butter, softened

1 1/2 cups granulated sugar

1/4 cup honey

4 large eggs

1 cup sour cream

3 cups all-purpose flour

1 3/4 teaspoons baking powder

1/2 teaspoon salt

12 fresh Black Mission figs, stems removed and quartered

2 tablespoons firmly packed brown sugar

Ginger Ice Cream (page 180) or Chantilly Cream (page 172)

The season for fresh figs is in the late summer and fall, but there is a brief time in the spring when they are also available. I call this my brainstorming period for figs. In early June, I whet my appetite for figs and start creating new desserts with them. When the short season ends, I put the ideas in the back of my head to simmer. Come fall, like a bear coming out of hibernation, I am ready to take full advantage of the main crop and produce a wide array of fig desserts. | Dried figs can also be used in this cake. Be sure to soften them in hot water or juice before adding them to the batter. This will prevent the dried figs from soaking up the moisture from the cake, which would make the cake dry. This recipe can be made for a dinner party, and the left-overs will be delicious served as an afternoon snack.

Preheat the oven to 350 degrees F. Grease a 9-inch Bundt pan and coat with the bread crumbs.

With an electric mixer, beat the butter until smooth, 1 minute with a stand mixer or 3 minutes with a handheld mixer. Add the granulated sugar and honey and mix until blended. Mix in the eggs one at a time, combining well between each addition. Stir in the sour cream.

In a separate bowl, or on a piece of parchment paper, sift together the flour, baking powder, and salt. On low speed, add the dry ingredients to the butter mixture and mix until combined.

In a small bowl, mix together the figs and brown sugar.

Spread one-third of the batter into the prepared pan. Place half of the figs evenly over the batter. Gently spread another third of the batter on top. Spread the remaining figs and then the remaining batter in the pan.

Bake the cake until a skewer inserted in the middle comes out clean, about 45 minutes. Be sure to test a couple of areas in the cake. If you skewer into a fig, the skewer will be wet.

Let the cake cool for 15 minutes. Unmold by placing a large plate on top of the pan, inverting the pan and the plate together, and then removing the pan. Let cool to room temperature before slicing. Serve with Ginger Ice Cream or Chantilly Cream.

PLANNING AHEAD: This cake can be made a day in advance; store well wrapped in plastic wrap at room temperature.

1/4 cup plus 1 tablespoon firmly packed dark brown sugar

2 large egg whites

Large pinch of cream of tartar

2 1/2 pints strawberries

About 2 tablespoons granulated sugar

1 1/2 cups crème fraîche (store-bought or homemade, see page 172)

brown sugar meringues

WITH STRAWBERRIES

Makes **8** servings

One of the advantages of living in California is that strawberry season starts much earlier than in other parts of the country. By mid-April, we have beautiful strawberries, while other parts of the country have to wait until at least May if not June. At Farallon we are all thrilled to have some bright red to balance the yellows and oranges of tropical fruits and the browns of nuts and chocolate, and we rush them onto the dessert menu. Here's a recipe that accents strawberries' delicate flavor.

TO MAKE THE MERINGUES: Preheat the oven to 225 degrees F. Trace eight 3-inch circles onto parchment paper, leaving at least 1 inch between them.

Sift or push the brown sugar through a fine-mesh sieve onto parchment paper to remove any lumps.

With an electric mixer, whip the egg whites until foamy, 30 seconds. Add the cream of tartar. Increase to high speed and add the 1/4 cup brown sugar, a tablespoon at a time. Whip the egg whites until very thick and satiny, about 2 minutes with a stand mixer or 4 minutes with a handheld mixer.

Place a 1/4-inch tip in a pastry bag and fill it with the meringue. Starting from the center of each circle on the parchment paper, pipe the meringue onto the circles, making solid coils. Sprinkle the remaining 1 tablespoon brown sugar over the meringues.

Bake the meringues for about 2 hours, until they easily come off of the parchment paper. To test if they are done, remove them from the oven and let sit for a couple of minutes. Then, using a metal spatula, try to lift them off the parchment paper. If they don't easily come off, return them to the oven.

Place the cooled meringues in an airtight container.

Hull and quarter the strawberries. Sugar to taste with the 2 tablespoons granulated sugar.

TO SERVE: Place some strawberries in the bottom of each of 8 bowls. Spoon some crème fraîche over the berries and top with a brown sugar meringue.

PLANNING AHEAD: The meringues can be made several days in advance and stored in an airtight container. If the container is not airtight, the meringues will get soggy.

Strawberries that smell fragrant taste better. Check the bottom of the strawberry basket before purchasing—the prettiest berries are often placed on top and the white-shoulder ones on the bottom. Luckily, the plastic baskets they come in make inspection easy.

bourbon milk shake

Makes **4** servings

It is unusual for me to create recipes where the primary flavor is hard alcohol. Even though my Louisville friends long preached to me about the virtues of bourbon, I was never a big fan. Then I found myself attending a reception at the Labrout and Graham Distillery in Kentucky, where I tasted Woodford Reserve Bourbon. It was delicious—I was amazed at the deep undertones of butterscotch and vanilla. I knew it would go beautifully with ice cream as the alcohol could be downplayed and its other flavors intensified. | This milk shake is the perfect refreshment for a spring day. Working outdoors, pruning trees or fertilizing the lawn, you can feel warm from your activity while still feeling cold from the temperature. The ice cream in this cools you down while the bourbon warms you up. The amount of bourbon in the recipe is quite mild but just enough to get you back outside to finish your chores. If you are a bourbon enthusiast, feel free to add more. Pour the milk shake into tumblers and serve in place of afternoon tea. Teatime will never be the same. If you want a larger portion, the recipe can easily be doubled.

$^1/_2$ vanilla bean or $^1/_4$ teaspoon vanilla powder

4 $^1/_2$ cups Vanilla Bean Ice Cream (page 179) or store-bought vanilla ice cream

$^1/_2$ cup milk

$^1/_4$ cup Woodford Reserve Bourbon or other high-quality bourbon

If using the vanilla bean, split it in half lengthwise and scrape out the seeds. Reserve the bean for another use. Put the seeds or vanilla powder in a food processor or blender. Add the ice cream, milk, and bourbon to the food processor and puree until smooth. Add a little more milk if you like a thinner consistency.

Serve immediately.

PLANNING AHEAD: Milk shakes must be made just before serving.

frozen lemon parfait

WITH LEMON GINGER AND CASSIS SAUCES

Makes **8** servings

Considering how frequently lemons pop up in desserts, it's a shame that the word *lemon* carries such negative connotations. No one wants to drive a car that's a lemon. In England in the 1800s, a lemon was someone with a sour disposition. But lemons make magnificent desserts with bold flavors. In fact, the number of lemon-dessert lovers is second only to that of chocoholics. The phrase "to make lemonade out of lemons" means to turn a situation around from something negative (sour) to something positive (sweet). But why settle for lemonade when you can have lemon parfait?

FROZEN LEMON PARFAIT

6 large egg yolks

I cup sugar

$^1/_4$ cup freshly squeezed lemon juice

Pinch of salt

Grated peel from I medium lemon

I $^3/_4$ cups heavy (whipping) cream

LEMON GINGER SAUCE

$^1/_2$ cup freshly squeezed lemon juice

I cup sugar

$^1/_2$ ounce unpeeled gingerroot, cut into several pieces

I tablespoon cornstarch

Grated peel from I medium lemon

CASSIS SAUCE

$^1/_2$ cup sugar

2 tablespoons water

3 tablespoons cassis liqueur

Grease the inside of a 6-cup loaf pan (about 5$^1/_2$ by 9$^1/_2$ inches). Line the pan with plastic wrap, making sure to press it into the corners of the pan.

TO MAKE THE PARFAIT: Whisk together the egg yolks, sugar, lemon juice, and salt in a stainless-steel bowl until combined. Set the bowl over a saucepan of just-boiling water. (The bowl should sit over the water without touching it.) Whisk vigorously until thick. Place the bowl over an ice bath (see page 28). Whisk occasionally until cold. Whisk in the lemon peel. In a medium bowl, whip the cream until soft peaks form. Fold the cream into the lemon mixture. Spread the parfait into the prepared loaf pan. Freeze until frozen, at least 4 hours.

TO MAKE THE LEMON GINGER SAUCE: Combine the lemon juice, sugar, and ginger in a small saucepan. Bring to a boil. Boil until the sugar is dissolved, about 1 minute. Put the cornstarch in a small bowl. Remove $^1/_4$ cup of the liquid, whisk it into the cornstarch, and then whisk the cornstarch liquid back into the pot. Cook over medium-low heat, stirring constantly, until the sauce thickens slightly. Strain and stir in the lemon peel. Refrigerate until cold.

TO MAKE THE CASSIS SAUCE: In a small saucepan, stir together the sugar and water. Bring to a boil and boil for 30 seconds. Remove from the heat and stir in the cassis liqueur. Pour into a small bowl and refrigerate until cold.

TO SERVE: Place a cutting board or plate on top of the parfait pan. Invert the pan and cutting board together. Remove the pan and carefully peel off the plastic wrap. Slice the parfait 1 inch thick. Cut each slice in half diagonally. Place 2 pieces of parfait on each plate and spoon some of each sauce around them.

PLANNING AHEAD: The parfait and the sauces can be made several days in advance and kept refrigerated. Let the sauces come to room temperature before serving.

caramel chocolate-chunk tart

Makes **8** servings

You might expect to use a mint leaf as garnish on this dessert. Many pastry chefs feel the need to have "a little color" on the plate, especially when the dessert is chocolate and thus brown. What's wrong with just brown? Fashion designers create clothes in solid earth tones and describe them using food names like "chocolate" and "caramel." This dessert is many shades of brown: the tan of the tart shell, the golden brown of the caramel, and the rich browns from both of the chocolates. Mint belongs on a dessert plate only if it is one of the flavors in the dessert.

1 cup sugar

3 tablespoons water

1 cup heavy (whipping) cream

2 large eggs

3 ounces bittersweet chocolate, chopped into $^{1}/_{2}$-inch pieces or large chocolate chips

3 ounces milk chocolate, chopped into $^{1}/_{2}$-inch pieces or large chocolate chips

One 9-inch prebaked tart crust (page 170)

Chantilly Cream (page 172)

Preheat the oven to 325 degrees F.

Stir together the sugar and water in a medium saucepan. Cook over medium heat until the sugar has dissolved, about 3 minutes. Increase to high heat and cook, without stirring, until the sugar is amber colored, about 5 minutes. Remove the pan from the heat.

Wearing oven mitts, slowly add one-quarter of the cream. Be careful, as the caramel will sputter as the cream is added. Using a wooden spoon or heat-resistant spatula, stir the cream into the caramel. If the cream sputters violently, stop stirring. Let the bubbles subside and then stir again. Carefully add the remaining cream. Stir until combined. Pour the caramel cream into a medium bowl or large measuring cup. Let cool for 15 minutes.

Lightly whisk together the eggs in a medium bowl and then whisk in the caramel cream.

Scatter the chocolate pieces in the bottom of the tart crust. Pour the caramel filling over the chocolate. Place the tart on a baking sheet and bake until set, about 20 minutes.

TO SERVE: Cool to room temperature before serving. Cut into slices and serve with Chantilly Cream.

PLANNING AHEAD: Like all tarts, this is best made and served the same day.

coffee chocolate towers

Makes **6** servings

Professional pastry chefs have access to a lot of cool gadgets and fancy equipment for creating their desserts. This can be frustrating for home cooks when they decide to make a recipe without the same tools. Individual stainless-steel rings fall into this category. While available at some specialty shops, they can induce sticker shock. Luckily, there are ways around this. Some pastry chefs use PVC pipe from the local hardware store. They cut them into approximately 3-inch-long rings and line the insides with plastic wrap. These molds can be refrigerated or frozen but not placed in the oven. For an even simpler method, use 6-ounce tomato paste cans; cut off both ends and you have reusable ring molds. An added benefit is if you make a huge batch of pasta sauce using the tomato paste. I keep red pasta sauce in the freezer and defrost it as needed. It is my favorite meal after I have been baking all day. And it is a terrific precursor to this dessert.

> Do not hesitate to melt the chocolate with the coffee. Many home bakers are fearful of adding liquid to chocolate, as they think it will make the chocolate seize. It can, but only when a very small amount of liquid is added. When a larger quantity is poured in, as in this recipe, there won't be a problem.

Indispensable Chocolate Cake, baked in an 8-inch square pan (page 176)

WHITE CHOCOLATE COFFEE MOUSSE
9 ounces white chocolate
$^1/_4$ cup strong coffee
2 teaspoons instant espresso or coffee powder
1 $^1/_4$ cups heavy (whipping) cream

CHOCOLATE GLAZE
$^3/_4$ cup heavy (whipping) cream
4 teaspoons corn syrup
1 ounce (2 tablespoons) unsalted butter
8 ounces bittersweet chocolate, finely chopped

Vanilla Crème Anglaise (page 175)
Candied Macadamia Nuts (page 180)

TO CUT THE CHOCOLATE CAKE: Run a knife around the inside edge of the cake pan and invert it onto a countertop. Peel off the parchment paper. Using a clean tomato paste can, cut out 6 circles of cake.

Line the insides of six 6-ounce tomato paste cans (see headnote) with pieces of parchment paper 7 $^1/_2$ by 3 $^1/_2$ inches long. Place the cans on a parchment-lined baking sheet.

TO MAKE THE MOUSSE: Melt the white chocolate, coffee, and espresso powder together in a medium bowl (see page 23). Whisk until smooth. Cool the white chocolate, stirring occasionally, to room temperature. In a large bowl, whip the cream until very soft peaks form. Fold the white chocolate into the cream. Divide the coffee cream between the prepared tomato paste cans. Refrigerate until firm, about 3 hours.

TO MAKE THE GLAZE: Warm the cream, corn syrup, and butter in a medium saucepan over medium heat until it bubbles around the edges, about 3 minutes. Remove from the heat and whisk in the bittersweet chocolate. Cool until the glaze has thickened slightly but is still pourable, about 15 minutes.

Place a chocolate cake circle gently but firmly in each can on top of the mousse. Remove the mousses from the cans, and place them, cake-side down, onto a wire rack. Peel off the parchment paper. Place the rack on a sheet pan lined with parchment paper. Carefully pour the glaze over the top of each of the mousses, letting it run down the sides. Refrigerate the towers until firm, at least 1 hour.

TO SERVE: Using a large metal spatula, place the towers on individual dessert plates. Spoon some crème anglaise around them and top with the macadamia nuts.

PLANNING AHEAD: The towers can be made a day in advance and kept refrigerated. Place the macadamia nuts on just before serving.

honey cream– strawberry parfaits

Makes **8** servings

5 ounces white chocolate

3 tablespoons honey

8 large egg yolks

1 ½ cups heavy (whipping) cream

2 tablespoons sour cream

2 ½ pints strawberries

For many years, you picked the clear, plastic, bear-shaped honey bottle from the grocery store shelf and that was it. Now there is a delightful array of honeys on the market, each with its own nuances. Honey varieties range from mild to strong with many in between. While I love all types of honey slathered on my toast in the morning, I prefer the more mild floral honeys for baking. Light golden in color, acacia, clover, and star thistle honeys all go well with strawberries.

Melt the white chocolate in a double boiler (see page 23). Whisk until smooth. Set aside.

Heat the honey to lukewarm. Place the honey and the egg yolks in the bowl of an electric mixer. Whip on high speed until thick, 1 minute with a stand mixer or 2 minutes with a handheld mixer.

Warm ³/4 cup of the cream in a heavy-bottomed saucepan over medium heat, about 5 minutes. Slowly whisk the cream into the egg yolks.

Return the cream mixture to the saucepan and cook over medium-low heat, stirring constantly. As the honey cream cooks and thickens, stir with both a whisk and a heat-resistant rubber spatula, switching back and forth between the two. The rubber spatula scrapes the cream off the bottom of the pan while the whisk keeps it smooth. Cook until thick. Remove from the heat and whisk in the melted white chocolate. Transfer the honey cream mixture to a bowl and cool over an ice bath, stirring frequently with a rubber spatula.

Whisk together the remaining ³/4 cup cream and the sour cream until soft peaks form. Fold into the honey cream.

Hull and slice the strawberries. Layer the berries and the honey cream in tall parfait glasses. Refrigerate until ready to serve.

PLANNING AHEAD: The honey cream can be made a day in advance and kept refrigerated. Slice the berries and assemble the parfaits within a few hours of serving.

HONEY

The flowers the honeybees visit determine the type of honey. Hives are placed strategically to take advantage of blooming crops and to control what kind of honey is collected. Honeybees fly within a one-mile radius of their hives to gather the nectar that they magically transform into honey. Once they stop at their first flower, they will continue to go to the same type of flowering plant as long as that nectar is within range. No mixing for honeybees. A beekeeper can identify single-source honey by its uniform color. USDA regulations require single-flavor honeys to have at least 80% of a particular variety. A blended honey is created when beekeepers mix different types or when various blooming crops are so close together that the honeybees collect more than one kind of nectar.

milk chocolate cheesecake

Makes **10** servings

On weekends when I am not baking, you can find me on my in-law's ranch tending the cows. Spring is roundup time. We rise at dawn, separate the cows from the calves, and rope, brand, and doctor the hundred-plus calves. By dinnertime, we are ravenous for the feast Mark (executive chef and co-owner of Farallon), the other Farallon chefs, and I prepare. After everyone takes a dip in the creek to wash away dust and ice-cold beers are passed around, I ring a triangular dinner bell. One year, prime rib, slowly cooked whole over a low fire for several hours, was the main dish. For dessert I prepared Milk Chocolate Cheesecake to combine two of ranch manager Kelly's favorite flavors. He always outworks us all and deserves a special dessert, not to mention the first piece.

CRUST

2 ounces (about 5) graham crackers

5 ounces (1 cup) whole natural almonds, toasted (see page 26)

1 1/2 ounces (3 tablespoons) unsalted butter, melted

CHEESECAKE

12 ounces milk chocolate, coarsely chopped

1 1/2 pounds cream cheese, at room temperature

1 cup sugar

4 large eggs

16 ounces sour cream

Chantilly Cream (page 172)

Candied Almonds (page 180)

Preheat the oven to 300 degrees F.

TO MAKE THE CRUST: In a food processor, finely grind the graham crackers and the almonds. Place the crumbs in a medium bowl and stir in the melted butter. Press the crumbs in the bottom of a 9-inch springform pan. Wrap the bottom and sides of the pan in a double-thick layer of aluminum foil.

TO MAKE THE CHEESECAKE: Melt the chocolate in a double boiler (see page 23). Set aside to cool to room temperature.

With an electric mixer, beat the cream cheese until smooth. Add the sugar and again beat until smooth. Add the eggs, one at a time, beating well after each addition. Stir in the sour cream and then the melted chocolate.

Evenly spread the batter in the springform pan. Place the springform pan in a large roasting or baking pan. Place the baking pan on the oven rack and carefully fill it half full of hot water. Bake the cheesecake for about 1 hour and 15 minutes, until it is almost completely set. To test for doneness, gently shake the pan. The cheesecake should jiggle evenly from the center to the edges.

Take the cake out of the water bath and remove the aluminum foil. Let cool for 20 minutes at room temperature. Refrigerate until completely cold, at least 4 hours to overnight.

Spread the Chantilly Cream over the top of the cheesecake. Run a small knife around the inside edge of the springform pan. Release the latch and remove the pan. Garnish with the Candied Almonds.

PLANNING AHEAD: The cheesecake can be made a couple of days in advance; cover well with plastic wrap and refrigerate. Within several hours of serving, spread the Chantilly Cream over the top and garnish with the Candied Almonds.

1 cup sugar

4 1/2 cups heavy (whipping) cream

Pinch of salt

3/4 cup ice wine

STRAWBERRY RHUBARB COMPOTE

10 ounces rhubarb, cut into 1/2-inch pieces

6 tablespoons sugar

2 tablespoons water

1 pint strawberries, hulled and quartered

ice wine ice cream

WITH STRAWBERRY RHUBARB COMPOTE

Makes **6** servings

I usually hate waiting in line, but an ice cream line is differ-ent. My favorite ice cream stand is Gray's in Tiverton, Rhode Island. On warm spring and summer days, the parade of hungry people extends into the parking lot. I use the wait to mull over all the possible flavors. Should I branch out and try something new like black raspberry or butter pecan? Or should I get my usual double scoop of mocha chip and peppermint? | I thought up this recipe while standing happily in line at Gray's. You will have to make it yourself, however, as it is not found at any ice cream stand. It incorporates ice wine, which is made by allowing the grapes to freeze on the vine or, more commonly, freezing the grapes briefly after they have been harvested. Vidal Blanc Ice Wine from Sakonnet Vineyards is delicious, as is Bonny Doon's Muscat Vin de Glaciere. This ice cream refreshes the way ice cream should, but it is also sophisti-cated and complex and thus provides a nice ending to a for-mal dinner party.

TO MAKE THE ICE CREAM: Warm the sugar, cream, and salt in a medium saucepan over medium heat, stirring occasionally, until bubbles form around the edges, 3 to 5 minutes. Pour the cream in a bowl and cool over an ice bath (see page 28). Stir in the ice wine. Refrigerate for 4 hours to overnight.

Freeze the cream in an ice cream machine, according to the manufacturer's instructions.

TO MAKE THE COMPOTE: Cook the rhubarb, 5 tablespoons of the sugar, and the water in a medium saucepan over medium-low heat, stirring frequently, until the rhubarb is soft, about 8 minutes. Transfer to a bowl and cool to room temperature. Stir in the strawberries and the remaining 1 tablespoon sugar. Store at room tem-perature until ready to serve.

PLANNING AHEAD: The ice cream can be made a couple of days in advance. For freshness, the strawberry rhubarb compote should be served the day it is made.

This recipe uses Philadelphia-style ice cream, which is made without any eggs, just cream and sugar. The other common style is French custard, which is made by cooking a custard of egg yolks, sugar, milk, and cream, chilling it, and then freezing it.

vanilla, caramel, and cinnamon-almond panna cottas

Makes **8** servings
(each variation)

While they have only been recently discovered here (instantly becoming wildly popular), panna cottas have always been a staple of the Italian dessert repertoire. Made from cream, milk, sugar, and gelatin, the recipe is very basic. Although *cotta* means "cooked," they are not actually cooked. The cream and milk are heated through so the gelatin can be mixed in. The trick is to have enough gelatin to get them to set, but not so much that they have a Jell-O-like consistency and end up tasting rubbery. | Once you get the basic proportions, you can adjust the flavorings and create any number of variations. Here is a basic panna cotta recipe with two modifications. Choose one or make all three for a panna cotta sampler. Each is unique and will help spark your imagination to create your own interpretations of this dish. All can be served with fruit or even on top of a thin brownie.

VANILLA PANNA COTTA

1 vanilla bean
3 cups heavy (whipping) cream
1/2 cup milk
1 tablespoon powdered gelatin
3 tablespoons water
2/3 cup sugar
Pinch of salt

CARAMEL PANNA COTTA

(Ingredients as above)
3 tablespoons water

CINNAMON-ALMOND PANNA COTTA

(Ingredients as above)
2 1/2 ounces (1/2 cup) sliced almonds, toasted (see page 26)
1 cinnamon stick

TO MAKE THE VANILLA PANNA COTTA: Split the vanilla bean in half lengthwise and scrape out the seeds. Heat the seeds and bean, cream, and milk in a heavy-bottomed saucepan over medium heat, stirring occasionally until bubbles form around the edges, about 5 minutes. Turn off the heat, cover the pan, and let infuse for 15 minutes.

While the mixture is infusing, gently stir together the gelatin and water in a small heat-resistant bowl. Let the gelatin soften, about 5 minutes. Place the bowl of gelatin over hot water until dissolved and clear, about 1 minute.

Remove the vanilla bean from the cream mixture. Stir in the sugar and salt, then whisk the gelatin into the cream. Let cool until warm, stirring occasionally. Pour the mixture into eight 4-ounce ramekins. Refrigerate until set, at least 4 hours.

TO MAKE THE CARAMEL PANNA COTTA: Follow the Vanilla Panna Cotta recipe but instead of adding the sugar to the cream, stir together the sugar and 3 tablespoons of water in a medium heavy-bottomed saucepan. Over medium-high heat, dissolve the sugar in the water. Increase to high heat and cook until the sugar is a caramel color. Remove from the heat and carefully add the scalded cream and milk, a few tablespoons at a time, to the caramel. Proceed as with the Vanilla Panna Cotta recipe.

TO MAKE THE CINNAMON-ALMOND PANNA COTTA: Follow the Vanilla Panna Cotta recipe but add the sliced almonds and the cinnamon stick to the cream mixture. Strain the cream before adding the gelatin. Proceed as with the Vanilla Panna Cotta recipe.

TO UNMOLD THE PANNA COTTAS: Run a small knife around the inside edge of the ramekins, invert them onto individual dessert plates, and remove the ramekins.

PLANNING AHEAD: Panna cottas can be made a day in advance and kept refrigerated.

rhubarb orange tart

Makes 8 servings

Rhubarb desserts are unjustly given a bad rap. In its raw form, rhubarb is not very appealing, as it is tough, fibrous, and bitter. But cooked with the proper amount of sugar, the inherent flavor of rhubarb is unleashed, and once you taste it, you will look forward to it being served. Rhubarb is frequently referred to as the "pie plant." This makes sense since cooked rhubarb and sugar is very thick, the perfect consistency for a pie. Serve this tart with Chantilly Cream or ice cream. Everyone loves both of these and it will reassure rhubarb neophytes before they take the first bite. | Rhubarb is either fieldgrown or hothouse grown. Field rhubarb is darker red in color with green leaves, while hothouse rhubarb is pale pink with yellowish leaves. I use the field rhubarb—it is not available year-round like the hothouse variety, but its more pronounced flavor is preferred.

14 ounces rhubarb

Grated peel from 2 oranges

3/4 cup sugar

Pinch of salt

1 1/2 ounces (3 tablespoons) unsalted butter, softened

2 1/2 teaspoons all-purpose flour

3 large eggs, lightly beaten

1 prebaked 9-inch tart crust (page 170)

Vanilla Bean or Ginger Ice Cream (pages 179–180) or
  Chantilly Cream (page 172)

Preheat the oven to 325 degrees F.

Cut the rhubarb into 1-inch pieces, discarding the leafy end. Cook the rhubarb, orange peel, sugar, and salt in a medium saucepan over medium heat, stirring frequently, until soft, about 10 minutes. Transfer the mixture to a bowl and let cool for 10 minutes.

Stir in the butter and the flour. Stir in the beaten eggs. Spread the rhubarb filling into the prebaked tart shell. Bake the tart until set, about 25 minutes.

TO SERVE: Let cool completely before slicing and serving. Serve with ice cream or Chantilly Cream.

PLANNING AHEAD: As always, tarts are best made and served the same day.

ICE CREAM BALLS
Ginger Ice Cream (page 180)
2 ounces ($^1/_2$ cup) sliced almonds, toasted (see page 26)

SAVARIN
2 $^1/_4$ teaspoons dry yeast
3 tablespoons warm water
2 $^1/_4$ teaspoons sugar
3 tablespoons warm milk
3 large eggs
1 $^1/_2$ cups plus 3 tablespoons all-purpose flour
3 ounces (6 tablespoons) unsalted butter, softened
$^1/_4$ teaspoon salt

SOAKING SYRUP
1 cup sugar
1 cup water
1 vanilla bean, split lengthwise and seeds removed
2 tablespoons Grand Marnier
$^1/_4$ cup freshly squeezed orange juice
1 tablespoon freshly squeezed lemon juice
Pinch of salt

vanilla almond savarin

WITH GINGER ICE CREAM BALLS

Makes **8 to 10** servings

Most of us are familiar with baba au rhum, a cylindrical yeast dough that is soaked in rum sugar syrup. Savarins are closely related to babas and are named after Anthelme Brillat-Savarin, French gastronome and author of *The Physiology of Taste* (1825). Savarins use the same dough but are made in ring molds, either small one-serving molds or one large enough to serve a group of people. I Used as an accent flavor for decades, vanilla is now a popular primary flavor in many desserts. It is an ideal central component for a savarin sugar syrup. Vanilla beans and good-quality extract are two of the more expensive ingredients used in baking but because of their stunning perfumed aroma, they are worth every penny and should never be scrimped on. I like to make my savarin in a single ring mold and present it at the table with the almond-coated ginger ice cream balls piled in the center. It gets rave reviews even before it is eaten.

TO MAKE THE ICE CREAM BALLS: Scoop out 8 to 10 medium-size ice cream balls. Place on a baking sheet and freeze until hard, 15 to 30 minutes.

Place the almonds in a small bowl. One at a time, place each ice cream ball into the bowl and completely coat it with nuts. Place the coated ice cream balls back on the baking sheet and freeze until ready to serve.

TO MAKE THE SAVARIN: In a medium bowl, combine the yeast and the water. Stir in the sugar and let sit for 10 minutes. Whisk in the warm milk and then the eggs. Stir in the flour and beat with an electric mixer until smooth, about 2 minutes. Transfer to a greased bowl and place the butter in small pieces on top of the dough. Cover the bowl with plastic wrap and let rise until doubled, about 1 to 1 $^1/_2$ hours.

When the dough has doubled, add the salt and mix by hand or on low speed using an electric mixer until the butter is completely incorporated.

Butter the inside of an 8-inch ring mold or a 9-inch Bundt pan. With buttered fingers, evenly spread the dough in the pan. (Alternatively, you can use a pastry bag and pipe the dough into the pan.) Invert a large bowl over the pan and let the dough rise until doubled, about 1 hour.

Preheat the oven to 350 degrees F. Bake the savarin until golden brown, 25 to 30 minutes. Let cool for 10 minutes and then remove from the pan. Continue to let cool on a wire rack.

CONTINUED

TO MAKE THE SOAKING SYRUP: In a small saucepan, stir together the sugar and the water. Place the vanilla bean and seeds in the pan. Bring the mixture to a boil and boil for 1 minute until the sugar has dissolved. Remove from the heat. Add the Grand Marnier, the orange and lemon juices, and the salt.

TO SERVE: Place the savarin on a large serving platter with a lip. Remove the vanilla bean from the syrup. Using a bulb baster or large spoon, continually pour the syrup over the savarin until the syrup is completely absorbed. Place the ice cream balls in the middle of the savarin. Present at the table and serve a slice of savarin with an ice cream ball on top.

PLANNING AHEAD: The savarin can be made a couple of days in advance and frozen. Defrost before soaking. Soak the cake with the syrup just before serving. The syrup can be made a day in advance and reheated. The ice cream balls can also be made a day in advance.

> Recipes that use vanilla beans sometimes call for scraping out the beans from the pod. The leftover pod can be infused in custards or you can make vanilla sugar with it. Put the pod in a container with granulated sugar—in a few days, you will have vanilla-scented sugar. If you want fine vanilla particles in your sugar, dry the vanilla bean at room temperature for a few days, grind it in a spice grinder, and then stir it into the sugar.

coconut pavlovas

WITH LIME CURD, GINGER ICE CREAM, AND PAPAYAS

Makes **6** servings

I knew Australian pavlova was the equivalent to American apple pie when I saw it on the menu at a McDonald's in Sydney. I like mine the way they serve them Down Under: crispy on the outside and a little chewy in the middle. Pavlovas are made of sugar and egg whites and tend to be on the sweet side, so be sure to use unsweetened coconut. It can be found in gourmet and health food stores. I also serve pavlovas with a citrus curd to cut down on the sweetness. Key lime curd works well—it has the same pucker-inducing qualities as other types of limes but its fragrance softens the overall taste.

COCONUT MERINGUES

3 large egg whites (reserve 2 of the yolks for the lime curd)

$1/8$ teaspoon cream of tartar

$1/2$ teaspoon vanilla extract

$3/4$ cup granulated sugar

$1^{1}/2$ teaspoons cornstarch

I tablespoon arrowroot

I teaspoon white vinegar

$1/2$ cup unsweetened shredded coconut

LIME CURD

6 tablespoons granulated sugar

$1/4$ cup freshly squeezed lime juice (see headnote)

I large egg

2 large egg yolks

Ginger Ice Cream (page 180)

2 ripe papayas, peeled and cut into $1/2$-inch pieces

Preheat the oven to 400 degrees F.

TO MAKE THE MERINGUES: On high speed, whip the egg whites, cream of tartar, and vanilla about 1 minute with a stand mixer or 2 minutes with a handheld mixer. Add the granulated sugar in a steady stream and whip until thick, about 1 minute with a stand mixer or 2 minutes with a handheld mixer. Fold in the cornstarch, arrowroot, wine vinegar, and the coconut.

Using a large spoon or ice cream scoop, spoon out 6 meringue blobs onto a baking sheet lined with parchment paper. Reduce the oven temperature to 300 degrees F. Bake the meringues until dry on the outside but a little soft in the middle, 45 to 50 minutes. Let cool and store in an airtight container.

TO MAKE THE CURD: In a stainless-steel bowl, whisk together the sugar, lime juice, egg, and egg yolks. Pour the mixture into a heavy-bottomed saucepan and cook over medium-low heat, stirring continually, until the mixture is thick, about 5 minutes. Pass through a fine-mesh sieve into a bowl, then put plastic wrap directly on the surface of the curd. Refrigerate until cold.

TO ASSEMBLE THE PAVLOVAS: Place a meringue on each of 6 dessert plates. Fill the middle of each meringue with lime curd, then place a scoop of ginger ice cream on top of the curd. Sprinkle papaya pieces on the plate around the pavlova. Serve immediately.

PLANNING AHEAD: The meringues can be made a day in advance and stored in an airtight container. The lime curd can be made a day in advance and kept refrigerated. Assemble the pavlovas just before serving them.

passion fruit soufflés

WITH MANGO SAUCE

Makes **6** servings

Wrinkly and unattractive in appearance, ripe passion fruits are nonetheless delicious. Cut them in half and scoop out the insides, seeds and all. There isn't much juice in passion fruit but its flavor is concentrated, so a little goes a long way. Passion fruits can be eaten right out of the shell, or you can puree them in a food processor to smooth out the texture. A quicker and easier way to obtain passion fruit puree is to purchase it (see the listing for Perfect Puree in Resources, page 182). | To prepare the mangoes for the sauce, first peel off the skin. At one of the ends, feel for the flat pit that runs almost the width of the fruit. With a large knife, cut off the flesh along the flat side of the pit. Repeat on the other side.

PASSION FRUIT SOUFFLÉS

- 3 large eggs, separated, plus 1 egg white
- 1/4 cup plus 3 tablespoons sugar
- 1/4 cup all-purpose flour
- 1/2 vanilla bean
- 1 cup milk
- 3 tablespoons passion fruit puree (see headnote)

MANGO SAUCE

- 2 mangoes (about 2 pounds total)
- 3 tablespoons sugar
- 1/4 teaspoon freshly squeezed lemon juice
- Pinch of salt

TO MAKE THE SOUFFLÉS: In a medium bowl, whisk together 2 of the egg yolks and the 1/4 cup sugar. Whisk in the flour.

Slice the vanilla bean in half lengthwise and scrape out the seeds. Reserve the pod for another use. Heat the vanilla bean seeds and the milk in a medium saucepan over medium heat until the milk bubbles around the edges, about 3 minutes. Whisk 1/4 cup of the milk into the egg mixture until smooth. Whisk in the remaining milk. Pour the milk mixture back into the pan. Cook, over low heat, stirring constantly with a rubber spatula, until it begins to thicken. Switch to a whisk and whisk until smooth. Switch back to the rubber spatula and continue to cook until thick like mayonnaise.

Transfer the cream to a clean bowl and whisk in the remaining egg yolk and the passion fruit puree. Place plastic wrap directly on the surface of the cream. Refrigerate until cold, at least 1 hour.

TO MAKE THE MANGO SAUCE: Peel the mangoes and remove the flesh from the seed (see headnote). Puree the flesh in a food processor until smooth. Strain through a medium sieve into a medium bowl. Whisk in the sugar, lemon juice, and salt. Refrigerate until you are ready to serve the soufflés.

TO BAKE THE SOUFFLÉS: Preheat the oven to 375 degrees F. Butter the insides of six 4-ounce ramekins and sprinkle with sugar. Whip the egg whites until soft peaks form. Add the 3 tablespoons sugar and whip until satiny and smooth. Gently fold half of the whites into the passion fruit cream until they are two-thirds incorporated. Fold the remaining egg whites into the passion fruit cream. Divide the soufflé mixture among the ramekins. Place on a baking sheet and bake for 8 to 10 minutes, until a skewer inserted in the middle comes out almost completely clean.

TO SERVE: Place each of the soufflés on a dessert plate and serve immediately with a small pitcher of the Mango Sauce on the side of each soufflé or a large pitcher for the table to share.

PLANNING AHEAD: The passion fruit–egg yolk mixture can be made a day in advance and kept refrigerated. The egg whites must be whipped and the soufflés baked just before serving. The Mango Sauce can be made a day ahead and kept refrigerated.

strawberry ginger sodas

WITH ORANGE SHERBET

Makes **8** servings

As a child I always ordered orange sherbet for dessert when we went out to restaurants. I had it on a cone at the Howard Johnson's counter on the way to my grandmother's house in Madison, Connecticut. At Pierce's Restaurant in Elmira, New York, a tuxedo-clad waiter presented me with my scoop in a sterling silver dish. As a pastry chef, I often use it in desserts. This ice cream soda with orange sherbet is loaded with strawberries. A little bit of ginger ale gives it a nice bright flavor and refreshing bubbles. | The nomenclature for sherbet can be a bit confusing: It is sometimes used as a synonym for French sorbet, which is composed solely of fruit puree or juices and sugar; sometimes it includes egg whites to make it fluffier; and many recipes, like the one here, add milk for a little creaminess.

ORANGE SHERBET

3 3/4 cups milk

3/4 cup sugar

Grated peel of 3 oranges

2 teaspoons freshly squeezed lemon juice

Pinch of salt

STRAWBERRY PUREE

6 pints strawberries

3/4 cup sugar, plus more to taste

Pinch of salt

I tablespoon freshly squeezed lemon juice

3/4 cup (one 12-ounce can) ginger ale

TO MAKE THE SHERBET: Warm the milk, sugar, and orange peel in a heavy-bottomed saucepan over medium heat, stirring frequently, until the cream is very hot and the sugar has dissolved, about 5 minutes. Remove the cream from the heat and stir in the lemon juice and salt.

Refrigerate the cream for at least several hours to overnight. Strain the milk and discard the peel. Freeze the sherbet in an ice cream machine according to the manufacturer's instructions. Place the sherbet in the freezer for several hours to overnight.

TO MAKE THE STRAWBERRY PUREE: Hull the strawberries. Puree them in a food processor until smooth. Transfer the puree to a bowl and stir in the 3/4 cup sugar, salt, and lemon juice. Taste the strawberry puree—if it is not sweet enough, add another 1 or 2 tablespoons of sugar.

TO SERVE: In a large pitcher, stir together the ginger ale and the strawberry puree. Pour the puree into 8 tall glasses. Place 3 small scoops of sherbet in each glass. Serve immediately with a long spoon and a straw.

PLANNING AHEAD: The sherbet can be made several days ahead. If it is very hard and difficult to scoop, place in the refrigerator for 15 minutes before scooping. The strawberry puree can be made a day ahead and kept refrigerated. Add the ginger ale just before you serve the sodas.

CRUST

   10 ounces (20 tablespoons) unsalted butter, softened

   1 cup sugar

   1 large egg

   3 1/2 cups all-purpose flour

FILLING

   1/2 cup heavy (whipping) cream

   1/3 cup milk

   8 ounces (2 cups) hazelnuts, toasted and skinned (see page 26)

   8 ounces (2 cups) coarsely chopped walnuts, toasted (see page 26)

   1 1/2 cups sugar

   5 teaspoons honey

   1 1/4 teaspoons freshly squeezed lemon juice

   5 teaspoons light corn syrup

   5 teaspoons water

   1 large egg, lightly beaten

walnut hazelnut bars

Makes **32** bars, each 2 1/4 by 1 3/4 inches

I'm a big fan of potluck parties. While the name still brings images of Jell-O salads and casseroles served in Pyrex, luckily what people contribute has changed over the years as our tastes in food have adapted. Perhaps we should give potluck a more current name. Having the guests bring most of the food is a tremendous time-saver for the host, who can then concentrate on creating the best possible party atmosphere. Potluck also lets people feel they contributed something and generates whispered conversation over who brought which dish. | Potluck desserts work best if they are finger food that can be eaten while holding a drink or cup of coffee. Cut the pieces small, so everyone can sample several items before getting full. Brownies, pecan squares, and cookies are the usual choices, but here is a recipe for something a little different.

Preheat the oven to 350 degrees F.

TO MAKE THE CRUST: Using an electric mixer on medium speed, cream the butter and sugar until smooth, about 30 seconds with a stand mixer or 1 minute with a handheld mixer. Add the egg and mix until combined. Stir in the flour on low speed.

Divide the dough into 2 equal pieces. Form each into a disk and wrap in plastic wrap. Refrigerate for 30 minutes.

On a lightly floured piece of parchment paper or wax paper, roll each piece of dough into a 9-by-13-inch rectangle. Place one of the rectangles in the bottom of a 9-by-13-inch pan. (If the dough is very soft and hard to pick up, refrigerate for about 15 minutes.) Refrigerate the second rectangle. Pierce the dough in the pan about 30 times with a fork. Bake until golden brown, 15 to 20 minutes.

While the crust is baking, prepare the filling: Mix together the cream and milk in a large measuring cup. Put the nuts in a medium bowl. In a medium saucepan over medium-high heat, cook the sugar, honey, lemon juice, corn syrup, and water until it is light caramel in color, about 5 minutes. Remove the pan from the heat and let the bubbles subside.

Carefully stir a couple tablespoons of the cream mixture into the caramel. Be careful, as the caramel may sputter when you add the liquid. Carefully stir in a couple more tablespoons. Stir in the remaining cream. Pour the caramel over the nuts. Stir, using a rubber spatula, until they are evenly coated. Let the mixture cool at room temperature, stirring occasionally, for 5 minutes.

CONTINUED

Spread the nut mixture over the crust. Place the second piece of (uncooked) dough on top of the nuts. Brush the top with some of the beaten egg. With a fork, make a decorative crosshatch pattern. Bake until golden brown, 15 to 20 minutes.

Let cool to room temperature. Run a knife around the inside edge of the pan to loosen the edges. Cut the bars lengthwise into quarters and crosswise into eighths, making 32 rectangles.

PLANNING AHEAD: The bars can be made a day in advance; store at room temperature, wrapped in plastic wrap.

apple filo napoleons

Makes **8** servings

When I design a menu for a party, I often select the dessert first and work backward. If I am in the mood for a rich gooey dessert, I will pick a lighter main course and sometimes omit a first course altogether. If I am craving a lighter dessert like this one, I can enjoy a richer first course or main course. You could serve steak au poivre or pasta with this apple napoleon. It goes with everything. After a meal, I do not want to leave the table hungry and wishing there was more, nor do I want to waddle away from the table and collapse onto the nearest couch. I want to feel just right.

APPLES

6 apples (Braeburn, Jonathan, Gala, or Golden Delicious)

5 tablespoons sugar

Pinch of salt

1 teaspoon freshly squeezed lemon juice

$1/4$ cup apple juice

FILO

2 ounces (about $1/2$ cup) pecans, toasted (see page 26)

$1/2$ cup sugar

4 sheets filo, defrosted (see page 25)

4 ounces (8 tablespoons) unsalted butter, melted

Cinnamon Cream (page 174)

TO PREPARE THE APPLES: Peel, core, and slice the apples $1/8$ inch thick. Cook the apples, sugar, salt, and lemon and apple juices over medium heat in a large sauté pan until the apples are soft but still retain their shape, 10 to 15 minutes, depending on the type of apple used. Transfer to a bowl and let cool to room temperature.

TO PREPARE THE FILO: Preheat the oven to 350 degrees F. Line 2 baking sheets with parchment paper.

Finely grind the pecans and sugar together in a food processor. Put in a small bowl. (If you do not have a food processor, very finely chop the pecans. Put them in a bowl and stir in the sugar.)

Lay the sheets of filo on a flat work surface. Remove 1 sheet from the stack and place it on the work surface in front of you. Cover the remaining sheets with a kitchen towel. Brush the single sheet with some of the melted butter and then sprinkle with a quarter of the pecan sugar. Lay a second sheet of filo on top of the first and again butter and sugar it. Continue in the same manner with the remaining 2 sheets of filo.

Trim the filo into a 16-by-12-inch rectangle. Cut into 3-by-4-inch rectangles. There should be 16 pieces. Using a metal spatula, place the filo rectangles, $1/2$ inch apart, onto prepared baking sheets. Bake until golden brown, about 10 minutes.

TO ASSEMBLE THE NAPOLEONS: Place a piece of the filo on each of 8 dessert plates. Place some apples and then some Cinnamon Cream on top. Place a second filo rectangle on top of the Cinnamon Cream. Serve immediately.

PLANNING AHEAD: The apples can be made a day in advance; refrigerate and let come to room temperature or reheat in the microwave before serving. The filo rectangles can be assembled the day before as well; place them in a single layer on a baking sheet, cover with plastic wrap, and refrigerate. Bake the filo rectangles the day you plan to serve them.

SUMMER DESSERTS   Freshly mowed grass, blueberries, distant thunder, cherries, slowly melting ice cream cones, no socks, watermelon, sticky humidity, plums, twilight, peaches, sunburned shoulders, shortcakes, fireworks, barbeques. These are the hallmarks of summer.

Summer, more than any other season, is not just a time of year—it is a state of mind. It is about feeling carefree, living in the moment, and spending as much time as possible outdoors. Even when it rains, we open the windows wide. We sit on the porch and watch the rain fall as though it were a mesmerizing movie.

Summer desserts should be as straightforward and relaxed as the way we spend our days. Maximizing outdoor time means spending minimal time in the kitchen. We want desserts that can be prepared relatively quickly, preferably in the cooler mornings or evenings. Luckily, nature has done most of the work already, so it is a simple matter to make sensational desserts.

Every summer when the peaches, plums, nectarines, cherries, blackberries, and raspberries arrive, I cannot help but be in awe of what nature has given us. Produce is at its pinnacle in abundance and quality. The fragrances of vine-ripened cantaloupes and juicy peaches are intoxicating. The most crucial thing to keep in mind when composing desserts from summer's bounty is to stop before covering up the natural flavors. The dessert is actually just a vehicle to show off the perfection of the fruit. Fruits are interchangeable in many of these recipes. See and smell what is bursting with flavor at your market or farm stand and take it home. First-class fruit always creates first-class desserts.

Even in summer, there is a place for chocolate, as long as it is done with a gentle hand, and this is the time of year when we really appreciate ice cream, perhaps the quintessential summer dessert.

66 apricot jalousie tart

67 best-of-summer shortcakes

69 berry crème fraîche cake

71 chocolate–peanut butter milk shake

72 bing cherry filo rolls with
    cardamom ice cream

74 black forest brownies with mocha ganache

75 cappuccino custard with cinnamon cream

77 candied ginger shortbread stacks with
    peach-blackberry compote

78 chocolate chip ice cream cake

80 lemon-raspberry bread pudding

81 mascarpone custard with summer fruits

82 corn crêpes with blueberry sauce and
    vanilla bean ice cream

84 peach blueberry trifle

85 pink plum granita with lime cookies

86 red berry white chocolate trifles

89 raspberry pie

91 three-melon sorbet bombe

93 rustic blueberry tart

95 white peach melba

1 pound, 12 ounces fresh apricots (about 14 medium), pitted
1/4 cup plus 1/3 cup sugar
1 3/4 ounces (1/2 cup) sliced almonds, toasted (see page 26)
5 ounces (10 tablespoons) unsalted butter, melted
8 sheets filo (see page 25)
Vanilla Bean Ice Cream (page 179)

apricot jalousie tart

Makes **8** servings

Most people assume that filo is difficult to work with. Once they actually use it, they happily discover that it is quicker and less intimidating than puff pastry and creates just as much flakiness. I am on a campaign to make filo an integral part of every dessert maker's repertoire. Jalousie tarts are traditionally made with puff pastry, so this is a perfect place to start. Jalousie tarts are also known as "peek-a-boo tarts," since the top crust has holes cut in it to reveal the inside filling. Serve this tart warm with vanilla ice cream—vanilla accentuates an apricot's flavor.

Of all the summer stone fruits, the apricot is the most underappreciated. Due to its shorter growing season, smaller crop, and the fact that it is not at its best eaten fresh out of hand, it will never match the popularity of the peach or the nectarine. But once you know how to maximize the full potential of apricots, you won't be able to resist putting some in your shopping cart next to the peaches.

The key to unleashing an apricot's flavor is to cook it, either on top of the stove or in the oven. In this recipe I do both. I blend some of the apricots into a puree and then fold it into the apricot pieces before baking the tart. An apricot's character blooms when it is heated, becoming juicy and fragrant. Cooking transforms even a mealy apricot into one with a smooth, soft texture.of nectar.

Preheat the oven to 375 degrees F. Line a large baking sheet with parchment paper.

Halve and pit 4 of the apricots. Cut them into 1-inch pieces. Place them in a medium pan with the 1/4 cup sugar and cook over medium heat, stirring frequently, until very soft and mushy, about 5 minutes. Transfer the apricots to a food processor or food mill and puree until smooth.

Cut the remaining apricots into eighths and put them in a bowl. Gently stir the apricot puree into the apricot pieces.

In a food processor, finely grind the 1/3 cup sugar together with the almonds. Put the mixture into a small bowl. Reserve 1 tablespoon of the almond-sugar mixture to sprinkle on top of the tart before baking.

Place the melted butter in a second small bowl. Unwrap the filo sheets and lay them flat on a work surface. Remove 1 sheet of filo from the stack and place it on a work surface. Cover the remaining filo with a kitchen towel, making sure it is completely covered. With a pastry brush, brush the single sheet with some of the melted butter and then sprinkle it with one-eighth of the almond sugar. Lay a second sheet of filo on top of the first sheet and again butter and sugar it. Continue in the same manner with 6 more sheets.

From one of the short ends, cut the filo into 2 rectangles, one 5 inches wide and the other 6 inches wide. Discard any filo trimmings.

TO MAKE THE BOTTOM OF THE TART: Transfer the 5-inch filo rectangle to the prepared baking sheet. (If necessary, trim an end of the filo to fit your baking sheet.) Spread the apricots over the filo, leaving a 1/2-inch border around the edge.

TO MAKE THE TOP OF THE TART: Using a 1 1/4-inch round cutter, cut 8 circles lengthwise and 3 circles crosswise on the 6-inch-wide filo rectangle, leaving a 1/4-inch edge around the outside of the tart. There should be a total of 24 circles. If you don't have a round cutter, cut slits 3/4 inch wide by 4 inches long. Holding the ends of the tart top, carefully pick it up with 2 large metal spatulas and evenly place it over the apricots. Press the top edge of the filo onto the bottom tart. Sprinkle the reserved tablespoon of almond sugar over the top of the tart.

Bake for about 20 minutes until golden brown. Let cool slightly before serving with Vanilla Bean Ice Cream.

PLANNING AHEAD: You can assemble this tart several hours in advance and refrigerate it. Bake the tart right before you plan to eat it for best flavor.

best-of-summer shortcakes

Makes **8** servings

The ingredients used to make shortcakes are the staples of the baking pantry: butter, sugar, flour, salt, baking powder, and cream. It is remarkable that such basic components can combine to create such a flaky, light, and buttery dessert. | The shortcake itself is just one element to a good shortcake dessert. What you serve the shortcake with is crucial. Select perfectly ripe fruits and above all do not add too much sugar. With summer fruits, nature adds most of the sugar for you, so you need to put in very little or none at all. Serve with Chantilly Cream and you have the ideal dessert for any summer meal.

SHORTCAKES

2 cups all-purpose flour

I teaspoon salt

6 tablespoons sugar

2 1/2 teaspoons baking powder

Grated peel of I lemon

3 ounces (6 tablespoons) cold unsalted butter

I cup plus I tablespoon heavy (whipping) cream

3 nectarines

3 cups assorted berries

Chantilly Cream (page 172)

Preheat the oven to 350 degrees F. Line a baking sheet with parchment paper.

TO MAKE THE SHORTCAKES: Combine the flour, salt, 3 tablespoons of the sugar, the baking powder, and the lemon peel in a large bowl. Cut the butter into 1-inch pieces and add it to the dry ingredients. Using a wire pastry blender, or the paddle attachment to an electric mixer, or two knives, cut the butter into the dry ingredients until the butter is pea sized. Add 1 cup of the heavy cream and stir until the dough comes together.

Place the dough on a lightly floured work surface. Pat or roll it out to 1 1/2 inches thick. Cut the dough, using a cutter or round glass, into 2 1/2-inch circles. Place the dough circles on the prepared baking sheet at least 2 inches apart. Using a pastry brush, brush the tops with the remaining 1 tablespoon cream and then sprinkle with 1 tablespoon sugar.

Bake the shortcakes until golden brown, about 35 minutes.

TO SERVE THE SHORTCAKES: If the shortcakes are no longer warm, heat them in a preheated 300 degree F oven for 10 minutes. While the shortcakes are baking or heating, peel the nectarines and cut them into 1-inch pieces, discarding the pit. In a medium bowl, gently combine the nectarines and the berries. If the fruits are not naturally sweet enough, add some of the remaining sugar, 1 tablespoon at a time, until the desired sweetness is reached.

Cut the shortcakes in half horizontally. Place the bottom of a shortcake on each of 8 dessert plates. Spoon some fruit and then some Chantilly Cream on top of the shortcake. Place the second half over the cream. Serve immediately.

PLANNING AHEAD: The shortcakes can be made a day in advance; wrap in plastic wrap and store at room temperature. Cut the nectarines right before serving to prevent discoloration.

berry crème fraîche cake

Makes **8** to **10** servings

I like going to the produce market and seeing rows of raspberry, blackberry, strawberry, and blueberry baskets. It reminds me that summer is in full swing. I know that these berries will be fragrant, plump, and juicy. Find berries at a farm stand and you are in for an even bigger treat. | In winter you can find high-priced half-pints of berries from New Zealand or South America among the apples and the mangoes. Unfortunately, the taste of these berries is often disappointing. For shipping purposes, they are picked before their optimal ripeness, drastically reducing their flavor and juiciness. Enjoy locally grown berries in summer when their taste is at their absolute best. In this recipe, I simply layer them in a poppy seed cake with some crème fraîche.

POPPY SEED CAKE

2 $^1/_2$ cups all-purpose flour

I teaspoon baking soda

$^1/_2$ teaspoon salt

I teaspoon baking powder

8 ounces (16 tablespoons) unsalted butter, softened

2 cups sugar

4 large eggs

I cup buttermilk

2 teaspoons vanilla extract

$^1/_4$ cup poppy seeds

CRÈME FRAÎCHE BERRY FILLING

I pint blueberries

$^1/_4$ cup plus 2 tablespoons sugar

2 cups (16 ounces) crème fraîche (store-bought or homemade, see page 172)

$^2/_3$ cup heavy (whipping) cream

I pint raspberries

Preheat the oven to 350 degrees F. Grease the bottom and sides of two 9-inch cake pans. Line the bottoms with parchment paper.

TO MAKE THE CAKE: In a medium bowl, sift together the flour, baking soda, salt, and baking powder.

Beat the butter with the sugar until light, 1 minute on medium-high speed with a stand mixer or 3 minutes with a handheld mixer. On medium speed, add the eggs, one at a time, beating for 30 seconds with a stand mixer or 1 minute with a handheld mixer after each addition. Periodically scrape down the sides of the bowl.

Stir together the buttermilk and the vanilla. On low speed, add half of the buttermilk. Mix until incorporated and then scrape down the sides of the bowl. Add half of the dry ingredients. Mix until combined and scrape down the sides of the bowl. Add the remaining buttermilk and the dry ingredients in the same manner. Stir in the poppy seeds.

Divide the batter between the two pans. Evenly spread it in the pans. Bake the cakes on the middle oven rack until a skewer inserted in the middle comes out clean, 15 to 20 minutes.

Cool the cakes in their pans for 10 minutes. Unmold the cakes by running a small knife around the inside edges of the pans. Place a plate or wire rack on top of each cake and invert the cake and plate. Remove the pans and let the cakes cool completely. Carefully peel off the parchment paper.

Using a serrated knife, cut each cake in half horizontally, making a total of 4 layers.

CONTINUED

TO MAKE THE FILLING: Cook the blueberries and 1/4 cup of the sugar in a small saucepan over medium-low heat, stirring often, until the sugar has dissolved and the berries have popped open and become juicy, about 5 minutes. Let cool to room temperature.

Whip together the crème fraîche, cream, and remaining 2 tablespoons sugar until stiff enough to hold its shape but is still smooth.

TO ASSEMBLE THE CAKE: Place a cake layer on a serving platter. Spread one quarter of the crème fraîche filling on top of the cake. Top with one quarter of the blueberry sauce and then one quarter of the raspberries. Place a second cake layer on top and spread crème fraîche, blueberry sauce, and raspberries on top as you did with the first cake layer. Repeat with the third and fourth layers, ending with berries on the top of the cake.

If not serving within an hour, refrigerate the cake. Once removed from the refrigerator, let it sit at room temperature for 15 minutes before serving for optimal flavor.

PLANNING AHEAD: The cake layers can be made up to 2 days in advance; wrap well in plastic wrap and store at room temperature. The blueberries can be cooked 2 days in advance and kept refrigerated. The crème fraîche and cream should be whipped just before assembling. The cake should be assembled the day it is going to be eaten.

If you don't use a lot of buttermilk and don't want to purchase a whole carton for this recipe, you can use dry buttermilk (which you mix with water), found in the baking aisle of the grocery store, or make sour milk by adding 1 teaspoon lemon juice to 1 cup milk. Stir and let sit for 5 minutes.

chocolate–peanut butter milk shake

Makes 4 servings

You must stay alert when ordering milk shakes. If you are in parts of New England and ask for a milk shake, you may be served a glass of cold flavored milk that has been mixed in a milk shake machine. It is frothy but does not contain any ice cream. It climbs quickly up the straw, a real disappointment when you are craving something thick and creamy. In these instances you need to ask for a "frappé" or a "frosted," or, if you are in Rhode Island, a "cabinet." Whatever you call it, it shouldn't move when you shake it. This milk shake is like a smooth Reese's Peanut Butter Cup. To add another burst of flavor, stir in some coarsely chopped Reese's Peanut Butter Cups just before serving and include a spoon with the straw.

4 1/2 cups heavy (whipping) cream
3/4 cup sugar
7 1/2 ounces bittersweet chocolate, finely chopped
3 tablespoons smooth peanut butter
1 1/2 cups milk

Warm the cream and sugar in a medium saucepan over medium-high heat, stirring frequently, or until hot and bubbling around the edges, about 5 minutes. Remove the saucepan from the heat and whisk in the chocolate.

Transfer the chocolate cream to a stainless-steel bowl and whisk in the peanut butter. Place the bowl over an ice bath (see page 28). Stirring occasionally, let cool until at least room temperature. Refrigerate until very cold, several hours to overnight.

Freeze the chocolate–peanut butter cream in an ice cream machine according to the manufacturer's instructions.

Place the finished ice cream in a food processor or blender, add the milk, and blend until smooth. Pour into tall glasses and serve immediately.

PLANNING AHEAD: The ice cream can be made several days in advance. Make the milk shakes just before serving.

2 ounces (about ¹/₂ cup) whole natural almonds, toasted (see page 26)

¹/₄ cup plus 2 tablespoons sugar

10 ounces (about 35) fresh Bing cherries

4 sheets filo (see page 25)

2 ounces (4 tablespoons) unsalted butter, melted

Cardamom Ice Cream (page 180)

bing cherry filo rolls

WITH CARDAMOM ICE CREAM

Makes **8** servings

Keep in mind that the cherry season is short—you'll want to take advantage of it as soon as possible. Get some the moment you see them in the market so you don't miss out. Although pitting may seem like a hassle, the results are worth it. Cherries have a pronounced flavor and pair well with strong spices. One of my favorite combinations is with cardamom. | When using fresh cherries, do not pit them too far in advance. Their flavor starts to dissipate and they turn brown soon after pitting. For small amounts of cherries, a single cherry pitter or paring knife works fine. For larger amounts, consider a cherry pitter of the feeder-plunger variety (see page 19). Whichever method you use, wear rubber gloves like those worn by food workers. Most drugstores sell them. Gloves will save you hours of scrubbing cherry stains off your hands and keep your guests from knowing what's for dessert before you tell them.

Preheat the oven to 375 degrees F. Finely grind the almonds and ¹/₄ cup of the sugar in a food processor. Place in a small bowl. (If you do not have a food processor, very finely chop the almonds. Put them in a bowl and stir in the sugar.)

Stem and pit the cherries. Cut them into quarters. In a small bowl, toss the cherry pieces with the remaining 2 tablespoons sugar.

Lay the sheets of filo flat on a work surface. Remove 1 sheet from the stack and place it on the work surface. Cover the remaining sheets with a kitchen towel. With a pastry brush, brush the single sheet with a quarter of the melted butter and then sprinkle with a quarter of the almond sugar. Lay a second sheet of filo on top of the first and again butter and sugar it. Continue in the same manner with the third sheet of filo. Place the fourth piece of filo on top of the stack but do not butter and sugar it.

Cut the filo vertically into quarters and then in half horizontally. You will have 8 rectangles. Place about 3 tablespoons of cherries on the end of each filo rectangle. Roll up the filo around the cherries.

Place the rolls, seam-side down, on a baking sheet lined with parchment paper. Brush the tops with the remaining butter and sprinkle with the remaining sugar. Bake until golden brown, 15 to 20 minutes.

Serve warm with the Cardamom Ice Cream.

PLANNING AHEAD: The cardamom ice cream can be made several days in advance. The cherry rolls can be assembled several hours in advance. Bake them right before you plan to eat them for the best flavor. They can be reheated but will lose some of their flakiness and crunch.

black forest brownies

WITH MOCHA GANACHE

Makes **16** 2-inch brownies

Many novice bakers begin to learn how to bake by making brownies. It is a simple and straightforward recipe to execute. But start a conversation with two pastry chefs on the perfect brownie and things get complicated very quickly. Cakey or dense? Nuts or no nuts? You will never achieve a consensus. Bakers, who all insist their brownies are the best, offer to bake you batch after batch but guard the recipe as if it were a classified document. Some will go so far as to keep the only record of it in their heads. This recipe (which I happily share) begins with my preferred rendition—fudgy, without nuts. I have added chopped cherries and a mocha frosting to turn it into a summer dessert appropriate for a dinner party or backyard barbecue.

BROWNIES

8 ounces bittersweet chocolate, coarsely chopped

I ounce unsweetened chocolate, coarsely chopped

4 ounces (8 tablespoons) unsalted butter

8 ounces (about 24) sweet red cherries, preferably Bing, plus 16 whole cherries with stems, for garnish

I $^{1}/_{4}$ cups sugar

3 large eggs

I teaspoon kirsch

$^{3}/_{4}$ cup all-purpose flour

$^{1}/_{4}$ teaspoon salt

$^{1}/_{2}$ teaspoon baking powder

MOCHA GANACHE

$^{1}/_{2}$ cup heavy (whipping) cream

$^{3}/_{4}$ teaspoon instant espresso or coffee powder

3 ounces milk chocolate, finely chopped

I ounce bittersweet chocolate, finely chopped

Preheat the oven to 350 degrees F. Line the bottom of an 8-inch square pan with parchment paper.

TO MAKE THE BROWNIES: Melt the chocolates together with the butter in a double boiler (see page 23). While the chocolate is melting, stem, pit, and cut the 8 ounces of cherries into eighths.

In a large bowl, whisk together the sugar and eggs. Whisk in the chocolate mixture and the kirsch. Mix in the flour, salt, and baking powder. Gently mix in the cut cherries. Spread the batter into the prepared pan.

Bake until a skewer inserted in the middle comes out almost clean but still with a little batter on it, 30 to 35 minutes. Let the brownies cool in the pan.

While the brownies are baking, make the mocha ganache: In a small saucepan, warm the cream and the instant espresso powder over medium-high heat until it bubbles around the edges, 3 to 5 minutes. Remove the pan from the heat and add the two kinds of chocolate. Whisk until smooth. Transfer the ganache to a small bowl. Refrigerate until firm, 1 to 2 hours.

TO SERVE: Cut around the inside edge of the brownie pan and place a cutting board on top of the pan. Invert the board and pan, then remove the pan. Carefully peel off the parchment paper. Cut the brownies into 2-inch squares. Place them, right-side up, on a platter. Using a whisk or electric mixer on medium speed, whip the ganache until thick. Frost each of the brownies. Place a whole cherry in the middle of each and serve.

PLANNING AHEAD: The brownies can be made a day in advance and stored wrapped in plastic wrap at room temperature. Refrigerate the ganache.

6 large egg yolks
2 large eggs
I cup sugar
Pinch of salt
2 3/4 cups heavy (whipping) cream
I 1/4 cups milk
3 tablespoons instant espresso or coffee powder
Cinnamon Cream (page 174)

cappuccino custard

WITH CINNAMON CREAM

Makes **8** servings

One of my favorite parts of a dinner party is near the end when guests are relaxing at the table over coffee, digesting the meal, and enjoying each other's company. In the middle of the summer, however, a hot cup of coffee isn't necessarily what one craves. To remedy this, on a warm night I serve a light fruit dessert followed by a mini coffee-flavored custard. This delivers the coffee flavor in a cool, refreshing way. A nice touch is to use ovenproof espresso or demitasse cups in place of the ramekins. Just before serving, top the custard with the Cinnamon Cream.

Preheat the oven to 300 degrees F. Place eight 4-ounce ramekins in a large ovenproof pan.

In a large mixing bowl, whisk together the egg yolks, eggs, sugar, and salt.

In a medium saucepan, warm the cream, milk, and espresso powder over medium-high heat, stirring frequently, until the edges start to bubble, about 5 minutes. Remove the pan from the heat and slowly whisk the cream mixture into the eggs and sugar.

Cool the custard over an ice bath (see page 28) until it reaches room temperature. Strain the custard. Carefully pour the custard into the ramekins. Slowly pour hot water into the pan so it comes halfway up the sides of the ramekins. Cover the pan with aluminum foil and carefully place it in the middle of the oven.

Bake until all but an area in the center of each custard, about the size of a quarter, is set. After 55 minutes, check the custards every 5 minutes to see if they are done. They may take up to 1 hour and 10 minutes. When the custards are done, take the pan from the oven and remove the foil. Let cool for 10 minutes.

Using tongs, transfer the custards to a baking sheet and refrigerate until cold, at least 4 hours.

TO SERVE: Serve cold with a small dollop of Cinnamon Cream.

PLANNING AHEAD: The custards can be made a day in advance and kept refrigerated.

candied ginger shortbread stacks

WITH PEACH-BLACKBERRY COMPOTE

Makes **6** servings

Blackberries can be deceiving. They may look juicy and ready to eat, but you won't know how sweet one is until you actually taste it. Tasting blackberries is a bit like jumping into a pool without knowing the temperature of the water. It could be refreshing or it could be a shock. Whether jumping into a pool or tasting blackberries, the method is the same, you just need to take the plunge. But jump you must, because the sweetness of the berry will tell you how much sugar you need to add. It is important to sweeten the blackberries before adding them to the peaches in this compote. If you combine the blackberries and the peaches first, you run the risk of oversweetening the peaches. Sweetening each fruit separately and then putting them together will give you the perfect balance.

CANDIED GINGER SHORTBREAD

4 ounces (8 tablespoons) cold unsalted butter

$1/4$ cup sugar

2 tablespoons candied ginger pieces (roughly $1/8$ inch each)

$3/4$ cup all-purpose flour

3 tablespoons rice flour

Pinch of salt

PEACH-BLACKBERRY COMPOTE

1 pint blackberries

2 tablespoons sugar, or as needed

$1/2$ teaspoon freshly squeezed lemon juice

Pinch of salt

1 pound (about 4) large ripe peaches

Chantilly Cream (page 172)

Preheat the oven to 300 degrees F. Line 3 baking sheets with parchment paper.

TO MAKE THE SHORTBREAD: Using an electric mixer on low speed, mix the butter, sugar, candied ginger, flours, and salt until they come together into a dough, 3 to 5 minutes. Form the dough into a 5-inch flat disk.

On a lightly floured board, roll the dough out $1/8$ inch thick and cut into eighteen $2 1/2$-inch circles. Combine and reroll scraps as necessary to get 18 circles. Place the shortbread circles $1/2$ inch apart on the prepared baking sheets. Refrigerate for at least 30 minutes.

Bake the shortbread until firm, about 30 minutes. To test for doneness, press the center of the shortbread with your finger. It should not be softer than the outer half. Let the shortbread cool to room temperature and then remove them from the baking sheets.

TO MAKE THE COMPOTE: Just before serving, place the blackberries, $1/2$ of the sugar, lemon juice, and salt in a bowl. Gently mix together. Taste for sweetness. If the blackberries are very tart, you may need to add a little more sugar. Peel, halve, and cut the peaches into $1/2$-inch slices. Taste for sweetness, adding 1 to 2 tablespoons of sugar, if necessary. Mix them in with the blackberries.

TO ASSEMBLE THE STACKS: Place a shortbread on each of 6 dessert plates. Place some fruit over the shortbread. Spoon some Chantilly Cream over the fruit. Top with a second shortbread, more fruit and cream, and finally a third shortbread. Spread any remaining fruit compote around the stacks. Serve immediately.

PLANNING AHEAD: The shortbread can be made up to a week in advance; store in an airtight container at room temperature. Prepare the cream within an hour or two of being served. Make the compote and assemble the stacks just before serving.

chocolate chip ice cream cake

Makes **8 to 10** servings

I have come to recognize that the perfect ice cream, like enlightenment, is always just around the corner, out of sight. But that's fine with me. I can spend my life searching. When I go to Italy, I strive to sample as many different *gelaterias* (ice cream shops) as possible. Obviously I can't try them all, so I have established some criteria to identify which are actually worth ordering in. It all comes down to the chocolate chip, or in Italian, *stracciatella*. If it has lots of chocolate chips in it, then I know it is a gelateria of high quality. If the stracciatella is mostly white with only a few brown specks, then I assume that it and all the other flavors are not worth tasting, and I walk fifty yards to the next gelateria. | Here is an ice cream cake recipe loaded with chocolate chips. The caramel sauce will not completely harden in the freezer. It becomes stretchy and very thick. | For even squares, I cut this into nine servings, a perfect amount for eight dinner companions and one to eat before everyone arrives. | While chocolate chip is my first choice for this recipe, feel free to substitute any flavor ice cream, homemade or store-bought. Just make sure the ice cream is of high quality. I prefer dense ice cream without a lot of air in it.

CHOCOLATE CHIP ICE CREAM

$^{1}/_{2}$ vanilla bean, split lengthwise and seeds removed

4 cups heavy (whipping) cream

$^{1}/_{2}$ cup sugar

5 ounces bittersweet chocolate, cut into chip-sized pieces

Indispensable Chocolate Cake (page 176), baked in a 8-inch square pan

Caramel Sauce (page 173), frozen for at least 6 hours

Candied Almonds, toasted (page 180)

TO MAKE THE ICE CREAM: Place the vanilla bean and seeds in a medium saucepan. Add the cream and sugar. Warm the mixture over medium-high heat, stirring occasionally, about 5 minutes, or until bubbling around the edges.

Transfer the cream to a stainless-steel bowl and cool over an ice bath (see page 28). Remove the vanilla bean. Refrigerate the cream for at least 1 hour to overnight.

Freeze in an ice cream machine according to the manufacturer's instructions. Fold in the chopped chocolate. Place the ice cream in a shallow baking pan and put it in the freezer to harden slightly, about 1 hour.

While the ice cream is hardening, remove the chocolate cake from the pan. Cut the cake in half horizontally. Clean the pan and line it with plastic wrap, making sure the plastic wrap fits into the corners of the pan.

Spread half of the ice cream evenly in the pan. Spread $^{3}/_{4}$ cup caramel sauce over the ice cream. (Freeze ice cream briefly if it gets too soft to spread the caramel.) Place a cake layer on top of the caramel. Repeat layering with remaining ice cream, $^{3}/_{4}$ cup caramel sauce and finally, the second cake layer.

Cover with plastic wrap directly on the surface of the ice cream and freeze until hard, several hours to overnight.

TO SERVE: Place a cutting board on top of the ice cream cake. Invert the board and the cake together. Remove the pan from the ice cream cake. (If necessary, wipe the bottom of the pan with a hot, wet, kitchen towel to help loosen it.) Carefully remove the plastic wrap. Sprinkle sliced candied almonds over the top of the ice cream cake. Cut the cake with a hot dry knife (see page 29).

PLANNING AHEAD: The ice cream can be made several days in advance. If it is too hard to spread, let soften slightly in the refrigerator for 15 to 30 minutes. The ice cream cake can be assembled a day in advance and kept frozen.

lemon-raspberry bread pudding

Makes **8** servings

Warm bread pudding is usually reserved for the winter months. Crusty bread soaked in a rich custard easily soothes both body and soul from the cold. It may not seem like a dessert for summer but when made with fresh berries it is an ideal ending to a meal in San Francisco. In this foggy City by the Bay, the temperature in July and August is often in the high 50s. You can easily forget it's summer unless you look at a calendar. Ten miles east, north, or south, the weather is much warmer, and an abundance of fruits grow throughout California. This dessert solves the conundrum of how to keep warm while highlighting California's gorgeous raspberries. If you don't find yourself in San Francisco, it is also comforting anywhere in the country during a thunderstorm. | Each time you have a couple of extra slices of bread left over, cut it into cubes and put it in the freezer. Before you know it, you will have enough to make this bread pudding recipe.

1 pint raspberries

8 ounces baguette, crust on, cut into $3/4$-inch pieces (about 4 $1/2$ cups)

2 $1/4$ cups milk

2 $1/4$ cups heavy (whipping) cream

$2/3$ cup plus 1 $1/2$ tablespoons sugar

$1/4$ teaspoon salt

Grated peel of 3 lemons

3 large eggs

3 large egg yolks

$1/4$ teaspoon cinnamon

Preheat the oven to 350 degrees F.

Evenly spread the raspberries into the bottom of a 9-by-13-inch pan. Place the bread pieces on top of the raspberries.

Warm the milk, cream, $2/3$ cup sugar, salt, and lemon peel in a medium saucepan over medium heat, stirring frequently, until the liquid is very hot and the sugar has dissolved, about 5 minutes.

Whisk together the eggs and egg yolks in a large bowl. Whisk the hot cream mixture, a little at a time, into the eggs. Pour the custard into the pan over the raspberries and bread pieces. Using a metal spatula, press the bread pieces into the custard, coating them with the custard.

Bake the custard for 40 minutes. While the custard is baking, combine the cinnamon and the remaining 1 $1/2$ tablespoons sugar in a small bowl. After 40 minutes, sprinkle the cinnamon sugar over the top of the bread pudding and continue baking until the tips of the bread pieces are golden brown and a small knife inserted in the middle is coated with thickened custard, about 10 more minutes.

Let cool at least 15 minutes before serving. Serve the bread pudding warm.

PLANNING AHEAD: The custard can be made a day or two in advance; refrigerate until ready to make the bread pudding. The bread pudding can be baked a day in advance. Keep refrigerated and reheat in a preheated 300 degree F oven for about 20 minutes.

mascarpone custard

WITH SUMMER FRUITS

Makes **6** servings

Mascarpone is one of the Seven Wonders of the World of food ingredients. A rich buttery cheese from Northern Italy, it became a staple in the American kitchen when tiramisu became popular. Everyone fell in love with this double cream cheese and has adapted it to many uses in both the savory and sweet kitchens. At 86% fat, what's not to love? I often add a little mascarpone cream when I am making Chantilly Cream. This creates a thicker and smoother cream with a superb texture. It also holds its whip longer than ordinary whipped cream. Although it has a generous amount of fat, a small amount is enough to please and satisfy the palate. This custard is an adaptation of the custard I put in my tiramisu. It is delicious served simply over peaches and berries. If you are nervous about using raw eggs, feel free to use pasteurized eggs (see Resources, page 182).

1/4 vanilla bean

2 large eggs, separated, plus 1 large egg yolk

1/4 cup sugar

8 ounces (1 cup) mascarpone

Pinch of salt

Pinch of cream of tartar

3 cups berries

3 large ripe peaches or nectarines, peeled, pitted, and cut into 1-inch pieces

Slice the vanilla bean in half lengthwise and scrape out the seeds. Save the vanilla bean for another use. Using an electric mixer, whip the vanilla seeds, egg yolks, and sugar on high speed until very thick, 2 minutes with a stand mixer or 3 minutes with a handheld mixer. Add the mascarpone and salt and again whisk until thick.

In a small bowl, combine the egg whites and cream of tartar. Whip until soft peaks form. Gently fold the egg whites, one-half at a time, into the mascarpone mixture.

TO SERVE: Place some of the fruits in each of 6 bowls. Spoon the mascarpone custard over the fruits. Serve immediately.

PLANNING AHEAD: The mascarpone custard can be made a day in advance and kept refrigerated. The peaches should be peeled and cut just before serving to prevent discoloration.

corn crêpes

WITH BLUEBERRY SAUCE AND
VANILLA BEAN ICE CREAM

Makes **6** servings

We were on a mission. It was the end of July and we were going blueberry picking in Rhode Island. At Little Compton's Boughs and Berry Farm we were provided with pails and ropes. The latter we used to tie the buckets around our waists, freeing both hands for more efficient gathering. Blueberries are one of the easiest berries to harvest—the high-bush variety stands about four feet and doesn't have prickly branches. An hour later, much to our amazement, we had picked forty pounds of blueberries! For the next couple of days, we had a baking frenzy: blueberry muffins, blueberry pound cake, blueberry pie, blueberry cobbler, blueberry pancakes, blueberry crisp, even blueberry jam. Everyone who came into the house, from neighbors to the UPS man, left with something blueberry. Believe me, forty pounds of blueberries are a lot of berries. I still had quite a few left. I needed to get creative and think up a new recipe. I remembered the Mexican tradition of using corn in desserts. Like blueberries, corn was at its seasonal peak, so it wasn't difficult to come up with a great-tasting dessert.

CORN CRÊPES

2 large eggs

1 cup milk

$^1/_2$ cup all-purpose flour

$^1/_2$ cup cornstarch

$^3/_4$ teaspoon salt

1 ounce (2 tablespoons) unsalted butter, melted

$^1/_2$ cup (about 1 ear) uncooked fresh corn kernels, preferably white

3 tablespoons white cornmeal, preferably stone-ground

BLUEBERRY SAUCE

1 $^1/_2$ pints blueberries

3 tablespoons sugar

1 $^1/_2$ teaspoons freshly squeezed lemon juice

Vanilla Bean Ice Cream (page 179)

TO MAKE THE CRÊPES: Put the eggs and milk in a food processor or blender. Blend until smooth. Sift together the flour, cornstarch, and salt and add it to the egg mixture. Blend until smooth. Add the melted butter and again blend until smooth.

Transfer the batter to a bowl and stir in the corn kernels and the cornmeal. Refrigerate for 30 minutes to overnight.

Heat a 6-inch crêpe pan or nonstick skillet over medium heat. Lightly grease the bottom of the pan. Fill a $^1/_4$-cup measure three-quarters full with the crêpe batter and pour it into the pan, rotating the pan so that a thin layer covers the entire bottom. Cook for about 1 $^1/_2$ minutes, until lightly browned. Using the edge of a knife, loosen a corner of the crêpe from the pan. Using your fingers, flip the crêpe over and cook for another 15 seconds. Place the finished crêpe on a large plate. Continue cooking crêpes, stacking them, slightly overlapping, on top of each other, until there are at least 12. It is not necessary to grease the pan after making each crêpe.

Wrap the crêpes in plastic wrap until ready to use.

TO MAKE THE BLUEBERRY SAUCE: Place 1 pint of the blueberries, the sugar, and lemon juice in a medium saucepan. Cook, covered, over medium heat, stirring frequently, until the blueberries are soft and juicy, about 3 minutes. Stir in the remaining blueberries.

TO SERVE: Place a small scoop of ice cream in the middle of each of the crêpes. Fold each crêpe over the ice cream. Lightly press the crêpes to flatten out the ice cream. Place 2 crêpes on each of 6 plates. Accompany with some warm blueberry sauce. Serve immediately.

PLANNING AHEAD: The crêpe batter and the crêpes can be made a day in advance; wrap in plastic wrap and refrigerate. The blueberry sauce can be made a day ahead. Reheat on top of the stove or in the microwave.

peach blueberry trifle

Makes **10** servings

The word *trifle* means "something of little importance." This definition, however, severely undersells what dessert trifles have to offer. The proportion of cream, cake, and flavorings is crucial in making a superb trifle. Too much cake and the trifle will be dry. Too much cream and it can be soggy. Too little flavorings and it can be bland. Here is a flavor combination that takes advantage of two of summer's best fruits: peaches and blueberries. Make sure that your peaches are fragrant and juicy and your blueberries are plump and you will have a terrific trifle.

BLUEBERRY COMPOTE

2 pints blueberries

$^1/_2$ cup sugar

8 large ripe peaches

3 tablespoons sugar, or as needed

2 cups sour cream

$^1/_4$ cup heavy (whipping) cream

Trifle Cake (page 178)

TO MAKE THE COMPOTE: Place half of the blueberries and all of the sugar in a small, heavy-bottomed saucepan. Cook, stirring frequently, over medium-low heat until the sugar has dissolved and the blueberries pop and give off some juice. Stir in the remaining blueberries. Let cool to room temperature.

TO ASSEMBLE THE TRIFLE: Peel and pit the peaches. Cut them into 1-inch slices. Roughly chop them by either placing them in a bowl and mashing them with a potato masher or processing them quickly in a food processor. Transfer the peaches to a bowl. Taste for sweetness and add up to 3 tablespoons of the sugar, as needed.

Combine the sour cream and cream in a medium bowl.

Cut the Trifle Cake into quarters and each quarter in half horizontally.

Place a large spoonful of the blueberry compote in the bottom of a 2$^1/_2$-quart glass bowl or attractive serving dish. Cut cake pieces to fit in a single layer over the compote. Cover the cake layer with a quarter of the blueberry compote, a quarter of the peaches, and finally a quarter of the cream mixture. Repeat layering all the ingredients 3 more times, finishing with the cream. (There will be a little cake left over.)

Cover the trifle with plastic wrap and refrigerate for at least several hours before serving.

PLANNING AHEAD: The blueberry compote can be made a day or two in advance and kept refrigerated. The trifle can be assembled a day before you plan to serve it and kept refrigerated.

The first time I made this trifle, it was for 30 people. That's quite a lot of peaches to peel. To speed things along, I blanched them for 10 seconds in boiling water and then immediately placed them in an ice bath to prevent them from cooking. After that, the peels slip off very easily.

pink plum granita

WITH LIME COOKIES

Makes **6** servings

A granita is an improved snow cone. The flavoring is mixed completely into the ice rather than just drizzled over the top. To create a vibrantly colored plum granita, I prefer Santa Rosa plums. The skins are pink-purple and the flesh is yellow with pink tinges. When cooked they turn a gorgeous bright pink. Other plum varieties will taste fine but may not have the same visual appeal. You can use this recipe as a base for any fruit-flavored granita; adjust the sugar according to taste. Serve this with a simple lime sugar cookie and you have a light and refreshing end to a meal. | On a hot day, the coarse ice crystals of a granita are more cooling than a smooth-textured sorbet. Unlike sorbets, making granitas does not require an ice cream machine, but just a shallow pan, a freezer, and a fork to create characteristic icy texture. With the luxury of the home freezer, it also does not require, as in Emperor Nero's time, slaves to collect snow from the mountaintops, run it down to the city, flavor it, and serve it before it melts.

PLUM GRANITA

2 $1/2$ pounds ripe pink plums (about 9), preferably Santa Rosa

I cup sugar, plus more as needed

Pinch of salt

I $1/4$ teaspoons freshly squeezed lemon juice

LIME COOKIES

3 ounces (6 tablespoons) unsalted butter, softened

$1/2$ cup plus 2 teaspoons sugar

Grated peel from I lime

I tablespoon freshly squeezed lime juice

$1/2$ teaspoon baking powder

$1/8$ teaspoon salt

I cup all-purpose flour

$1/8$ teaspoon ground ginger

TO MAKE THE GRANITA: Halve each plum and discard the pit. Cut each half into 4 pieces. In a covered medium saucepan over medium heat, cook the plums, $1/2$ cup of the sugar, and the salt, stirring occasionally, for 10 minutes. Remove the lid and continue to cook for another 5 minutes, until the plums are completely soft.

Let the plums cool to room temperature. Puree them in a food processor or through a food mill. Strain the puree into a bowl and discard the skins.

Whisk the remaining $1/2$ cup sugar and the lemon juice into the plum puree. If necessary, add sugar, a tablespoon at a time, until the desired sweetness is reached. Pour the plum puree in a shallow baking pan and place in the freezer for 1 hour.

Remove the pan from the freezer. Using a fork, mix up the puree. Continue freezing and mixing the puree in 30-minute intervals until it is completely frozen.

TO MAKE THE COOKIES: Preheat the oven to 350 degrees F. Line 2 baking sheets with parchment paper.

Using an electric mixer, beat the butter, $1/2$ cup of the sugar, and the lime peel on medium speed until light and smooth, about 30 seconds with a stand mixer or 1 minute with a handheld mixer. On low speed, stir in the lime juice and then the baking powder, salt, and flour.

On a lightly floured work surface, roll the cookie dough into 2 logs, each 10 inches long and 1 inch wide. Refrigerate until hard, at least 30 minutes.

Slice the cookies $1/2$ inch thick. Place them 1 inch apart on the prepared baking sheets. In a small bowl, mix together the remaining 2 teaspoons sugar and the ginger. Sprinkle the ginger sugar over the cookies. Bake until lightly golden, 12 to 15 minutes. Let cool and then remove from the baking sheets.

PLANNING AHEAD: The cookie dough can be made a day before serving and kept refrigerated. The cookies should be baked the day you serve them. For maximum flavor, the plum granita should not be made more than a day in advance of serving.

red berry–
white chocolate trifles

Makes **6** servings

"It's the berries" was one of my grandmother's favorite expressions. Dating from the 1900s, this phrase described something popular and cool. How is the movie? It's the berries. Do you like her dress? It's the berries. How is your dinner? It's the berries. After one bite of this trifle, you too will be saying, "It's the berries." If you can find fraises de bois, use them to decorate the top of the trifle.

Trifle Cake (page 178)

WHITE CHOCOLATE MOUSSE

4 large egg yolks

$^{1}/_{4}$ cup sugar

3 tablespoons Grand Marnier

3 tablespoons water

$1^{1}/_{2}$ teaspoons freshly squeezed lemon juice

3 ounces white chocolate, finely chopped

I cup heavy (whipping) cream

BERRY SAUCE

12 ounces frozen strawberries or raspberries (no sugar added), defrosted

2 tablespoons sugar, or as needed

I pint strawberries

I pint raspberries

I tablespoon sugar, or as needed

TO MAKE THE MOUSSE: Whisk together the egg yolks and the sugar in a medium stainless-steel mixing bowl. Stir in the Grand Marnier, water, and lemon juice. Set the bowl over a pot of simmering water, making sure the bottom of it does not touch the water. Whisk the eggs briskly until thick and the mixture has tripled in volume, 2 to 3 minutes.

Remove the bowl from the stove and whisk in the white chocolate until smooth. Let cool to room temperature, stirring occasionally.

Whip the cream until soft peaks form, then fold it into the white chocolate.

TO MAKE THE SAUCE: Puree the frozen berries in a food processor or pass through a food mill. Strain the puree through a fine-mesh sieve, discarding the seeds. Stir in the sugar. Add another 1 or 2 tablespoons of sugar if the sauce isn't sweet enough.

TO ASSEMBLE THE TRIFLE: Run a knife around the inside edge of the cake pan and invert it onto a counter. Carefully peel off the parchment paper. Cut the cake into quarters. Cut each piece in half horizontally.

Hull and quarter the strawberries; cut them into sixths if they are big. In a medium bowl, gently stir them together with half of the raspberries and the sugar. Taste the berries—if they are not sweet enough, add another tablespoon of sugar.

CONTINUED

Place a spoonful of berries in the bottom of 6 individual parfait or wine glasses. Spread a layer of the White Chocolate Mousse over the berries. Cut cake pieces to fit in a single layer over the cream. Spread some Berry Sauce over the cake, completely covering it. Continue layering more berries, mousse, cake, and sauce until you finish with a layer of mousse on top. There will be leftover cake. Freeze for another use. Arrange the remaining raspberries around the top of the trifles. Refrigerate the trifles for several hours before serving.

PLANNING AHEAD: The White Chocolate Mousse can be made a day ahead and kept refrigerated. The berry sauce can be made 2 days in advance and kept refrigerated. The trifle can be assembled a day before it is to be served and kept refrigerated.

When sieving berry sauce, use the back of a small ladle to push the sauce through. This works faster than a rubber spatula or whisk.

raspberry pie

Makes **8** servings

I am usually a pretty relaxed person, but when it comes to purchasing raspberries, I am, well, picky. They should have a deep red color, be soft not seedy, and dissolve sweetly in the mouth. I am happy when I find "squished" raspberries— I often feel a little guilty using perfectly formed raspberries for pies. Squished raspberries have great flavor and aroma and are perfect for pie. With squished raspberries, I can have my pie and eat it, too. Raspberry pies do not need much flavor enhancement—a little lemon and vanilla will do the trick. Avoid spices, as they will dominate the pie and overwhelm the raspberries' perfume. Serve with either vanilla ice cream or Chantilly Cream, whichever you prefer.

6 cups (about 1 pound, 10 ounces) fresh raspberries
1 cup plus 1 tablespoon sugar
1 teaspoon freshly squeezed lemon juice
$^1/_4$ cup all-purpose flour
Grated peel from 1 lemon
Pinch of salt
One 9-inch prebaked pie crust with unbaked lattice (page 170)
1 tablespoon heavy (whipping) cream
Vanilla Bean Ice Cream (page 179) or Chantilly Cream (page 172)

Preheat the oven to 350 degrees F.

In a large bowl, gently stir together the raspberries, 1 cup of the sugar, the lemon juice, the flour, the lemon peel, and the salt.

Place the raspberry mixture in the prebaked pie crust. Arrange the lattice on top of the pie in a crisscross pattern. Using a pastry brush, brush the cream on top of the lattice. Sprinkle the remaining 1 tablespoon sugar over the lattice.

Bake until the lattice is golden and the juices of the pie have thickened, about 50 minutes.

Let the pie cool to lukewarm or room temperature before serving. It will continue to absorb liquid as it cools. Serve with Vanilla Bean Ice Cream or Chantilly Cream.

PLANNING AHEAD: This pie is best prepared and eaten the same day.

three-melon sorbet bombe

Makes **8** servings

A frozen "bombe" is layers of different flavors of sorbet or ice cream prepared in a mold. In the late 1800s and early 1900s, bombe molds were tall, spherical, and often elaborate. Elizabeth David's book *Harvest of the Cold Months* shows pictures of bombes in the shape of pineapples, turbans, snowmen, baskets of oranges, and even windmills. Although this sorbet bombe recipe is made in a loaf pan and may not be as flashy when you present it at the table, it is colorful and the flavor is very refreshing. Cantaloupe, honeydew, and watermelon are layered to create a striped bombe. Melon balls are arranged on top for garnish and added flavor. If you have an ice cream machine with an insert that you must freeze before churning the sorbet, make sure to allow for several days to freeze all three layers. You can make the sugar syrup in advance, but for maximum flavor, cut and puree each type of melon the day you are going to freeze it.

SUGAR SYRUP

2 cups water

1 1/2 cups sugar

1/2 cup corn syrup

CANTALOUPE SORBET

one 2 pound cantaloupe

3/4 cup sugar syrup, or as needed

1 teaspoon freshly squeezed lemon juice

1/4 teaspoon salt

1 tablespoon vodka

WATERMELON SORBET

one 3 pound, 3 ounce watermelon

3/4 cup sugar syrup, or as needed

1 teaspoon freshly squeezed lemon juice

1/4 teaspoon salt

1 tablespoon vodka

HONEYDEW SORBET

one 2 pound, 8 ounce honeydew melon

3/4 cup sugar syrup, or as needed

1 teaspoon freshly squeezed lemon juice

1/4 teaspoon salt

1 tablespoon vodka

14 melon balls each of cantaloupe, watermelon, and honeydew

TO PREPARE THE LOAF PAN: Spray a 10-by-5-by-3-inch loaf pan with cooking oil spray. Line it with plastic wrap, making sure to press the plastic wrap into the corners.

TO MAKE THE SUGAR SYRUP: Cook the water, sugar, and corn syrup in a medium saucepan over high heat, stirring occasionally, until it comes to a boil. Boil for 1 minute. Transfer to a bowl or large measuring cup and refrigerate until cold.

TO MAKE THE CANTALOUPE SORBET: Using a knife, remove the cantaloupe flesh from the rind. Puree the flesh in a food processor or pass through a food mill. Strain the puree through a medium sieve into a bowl. There should be 2 cups of puree. Stir the sugar syrup, lemon juice, salt, and vodka into the puree. Taste for sweetness. Add another 1 or 2 tablespoons of sugar syrup if needed. Refrigerate for several hours to overnight.

Freeze the sorbet in an ice cream machine according to the manufacturer's instructions. When the sorbet finishes freezing, spread it in the bottom of the loaf pan. Place in the freezer.

CONTINUED

TO MAKE THE WATERMELON SORBET: Proceed as with the cantaloupe recipe, substituting watermelon for the cantaloupe. There should be 2 cups of puree. Freeze the watermelon puree according to the manufacturer's instructions. When frozen, spread on top of the cantaloupe sorbet.

TO MAKE THE HONEYDEW SORBET: Proceed as with the cantaloupe recipe, substituting honeydew for the cantaloupe. There should be 2 cups of puree. Freeze the honeydew puree according to the manufacturer's instructions. When frozen, spread over the watermelon sorbet. Freeze the terrine for several hours until hard.

Once frozen, invert the terrine onto a cutting board. Remove the pan. (If necessary, run a hot towel over the pan to help loosen the bombe.) Carefully remove the plastic wrap.

TO SERVE: Just before serving, arrange the melon balls on top of the bombe. Present it at the table before slicing. Serve each piece with some of the melon balls.

PLANNING AHEAD: The bombe can be made several days in advance. The melon balls can be made a day in advance; wrap well in plastic wrap and refrigerate.

The vodka is added to keep the sorbet from freezing really hard. It doesn't alter the favor—it is tasteless. Use a little vodka in any sorbet that has a watery fruit like pineapple or citrus.

rustic blueberry tart

Makes **6** servings

To make this rustic tart, you need only a generic baking pan and something to roll with. "Something to roll with" is not limited to rolling pins. Many times in a pinch I have used an empty wine bottle as a rolling pin when making this tart at friend's houses. You can use a full bottle of wine, but make sure it has not been refrigerated or the condensation will make the dough wet. You should also take care not to use a bottle that has been gently placed in the wine cellar to age. You may not get invited over again. Blueberries are a good choice for tarts because their high pectin content, compared to that of strawberries, for example, makes for a nice thick filling without having to add a lot of thickener. Before placing the tart in the oven, I scatter small pieces of dough over the top of it. This gives it some top crust and makes use of some of the scraps.

TART DOUGH

2 cups all-purpose flour

3 tablespoons sugar

Pinch of salt

6 ounces (12 tablespoons) cold unsalted butter

$^1/_4$ cup heavy (whipping) cream

1 large egg

$^1/_2$ teaspoon vanilla extract

BLUEBERRY FILLING

1 pint blueberries

$^1/_4$ cup sugar

2 tablespoons all-purpose flour

Pinch of salt

Grated peel of 1 lemon

Vanilla Bean or Cinnamon Ice Cream (page 179–180)

Preheat the oven to 375 degrees F.

TO MAKE THE TART DOUGH: Combine the flour, sugar, and salt in a large bowl. Using a pastry blender or two knives, cut in the butter until it is pea sized. In a small bowl, whisk together the cream, egg, and vanilla. Stir the cream mixture into the flour and butter. Stir until the dough comes together.

Form the dough into a 5-inch flat disk. Wrap in plastic wrap and refrigerate for at least 1 hour.

On a lightly floured piece of parchment paper or foil, roll the dough out to $^3/_8$ inch thick. Trim it into an 11-inch circle. Reserve about 2 tablespoons of the dough scraps.

TO MAKE THE FILLING AND FORM THE TART: Put the blueberries, sugar, flour, salt, and lemon peel in a medium bowl. Stir until combined. Place the blueberry mixture in the middle of the tart, leaving a 1-inch border around the outside edge of the dough. Fold the edge of the tart over the blueberries. Using some of the reserved scraps of dough, place about eight $^1/_2$- to 1-inch pieces evenly over the tart.

Carefully pick up the parchment paper by both ends and transfer the tart and parchment paper to a baking sheet. Bake the tart until it is golden brown and the blueberry liquid has thickened slightly, about 30 minutes. Let cool for 5 minutes before serving. Serve with the ice cream.

PLANNING AHEAD: The dough can be made and rolled several days in advance and kept refrigerated. The tart can be rolled and formed the morning of the day you plan to serve it; refrigerate until you are ready to bake it. This tart is best served warm. Once baked, store at room temperature. Reheat in a preheated 350 degree F oven for 10 to 15 minutes.

white peach melba

Makes **8** servings

Many people are aware that peach melba, composed of peaches, vanilla ice cream, and raspberry sauce, was named after the Australian opera singer Nellie Melba. What people may not know is that the classical chef Auguste Escoffier created this dessert. In his lifetime, Escoffier created many dishes in the names of famous actresses and singers. Considering that he lived in the 1800s, Escoffier's recognition of women was impressive. I wonder if they each had a peaches and-cream complexion or thought it was peachy keen that they had dishes created in their honor. This recipe is in tribute to Escoffier and is an adaptation of his famous peach melba. I have used the original flavors but combined them in a new way with baked peaches and raspberry granita.

> The secret to maintaining the striking perfume and taste of a perfectly ripe peach is to take special care once you bring it home from the store. Leave it on the counter until you are ready to use it: refrigeration will dull its flavor and aroma. Buy peaches where you can taste a sample and select ripe ones. Nothing is as depressing as placing a hard peach on the countertop, patiently waiting for it to ripen, and then having it either get mealy or develop a shriveled skin while the flesh never softens.

RASPBERRY GRANITA

12 ounces frozen raspberries (no sugar added), defrosted

1/4 cup sugar

6 tablespoons water

1/2 teaspoon freshly squeezed lemon juice

Pinch of salt

BAKED PEACHES

3/4 cup Moscato d'Asti

1/2 vanilla bean

4 large, ripe white peaches

1 tablespoon sugar

Chantilly Cream (page 172)

TO MAKE THE GRANITA: Puree the raspberries in a food processor or through a food mill. Strain the puree through a fine-mesh sieve, discarding the seeds. Put the puree in a medium bowl and stir in the sugar, water, lemon juice, and salt. Pour the sweetened raspberry puree in a shallow baking pan and freeze for 1 hour.

Remove the pan from the freezer. Using a fork, mix up the raspberry puree. This will give the granita an icy texture. Continue freezing and mixing the puree in 30-minute intervals until it is completely frozen.

TO MAKE THE PEACHES: Preheat the oven to 400 degrees F. Place the Moscato d'Asti in a medium bowl. Cut the vanilla bean in half lengthwise. Scrape out the seeds and stir them into the Moscato d'Asti. Save the vanilla bean for another use.

Peel the peaches, cut them in half, and discard the pits. Slice a little bit off the bottom of each peach half so they will stay upright during baking. Place the peach halves in the bowl with the Moscato d'Asti. Spoon the liquid over them to coat them on all sides. Let sit for 10 minutes, turn them over, and let sit for another 10 minutes.

Place the peach halves in a single layer, bottoms down, in a baking pan. Sprinkle the sugar over the tops of the peaches. Bake the peaches for 20 minutes (a few minutes less if the peaches are very ripe). Let cool to room temperature.

While the peaches are baking, place the peach soaking liquid in a small saucepan. Cook over medium heat to reduce until slightly syrupy, about 1/3 cup. Let the peaches and the sauce cool to room temperature.

TO SERVE: Place a peach half, pit-side up, on each of 8 dessert plates. Spoon some raspberry granita on top of the peaches. Dollop a little Chantilly Cream over the granita and drizzle syrup around the peaches. Serve immediately.

PLANNING AHEAD: The raspberry granita can be made several days in advance. The peaches should be prepared the day they are to be served.

AUTUMN DESSERTS We know it is autumn when apples and figs appear at farmers' markets, yellow and red leaves drift across the yard, and vivid orange pumpkins appear on doorsteps. The first frost ends our supply of vine-ripened tomatoes, and we need to pull on sweaters in the afternoon as the shadows shorten. Summer has ended.

But although the days are getting shorter, for me autumn is the beginning of a new year. The period from Labor Day, the symbolic end of summer, to the first calendar day of fall in the middle of September is when I shift gears. After a summer of relaxing and living in the moment, I am energized to take on new projects in the kitchen, happily experimenting, creating, and producing.

Fall produce possesses more earthy colors. Persimmons, figs, cranberries, and nuts are rich in hue, both in their natural state and when baked in desserts. They are also more sophisticated and robust in flavor than those that preceded them in summer. Luckily, raspberries like cool weather, so this berry extends its season a little longer. In autumn, apples and pears are in full swing. These are more adaptable in baking than other fruits. Served whole in Apple Splits (page 102), in pieces for Cinnamon Apple Crêpes (page 104), or pureed for Pear–Caramel Swirl Ice Cream (page 117), they produce strikingly diverse desserts. A marriage of any form of fall fruits with caramel is a matchmaker's dream. Chocolate emerges more in this season as well.

98   apple–olive oil cake

99   autumn "summer" pudding

101   raspberry–honey cream tartlets

102   apple splits

104   cinnamon apple crêpes

107   french plum tart

108   individual german chocolate cakes

110   orange marmalade tart

111   triple-layer pear brioche sandwiches

112   grandmother's apple cake

114   orange pound cake with concord
      grape compote

115   persimmon rum mousse with crème fraîche
      and caramel sauce

117   pear–caramel swirl ice cream with
      pecan cookies

119   figamaroles

120   pumpkin upside-down cake with cranberry
      pecan topping

122   pumpkin zuccotto

125   fig galettes with cinnamon marsala sabayon

127   ricotta cheesecake with dried cherries and
      golden raisins

129   walnut cake with chocolate orange sabayon
      and vanilla crème anglaise

131   walnut shortcakes with baked quince

apple–olive oil cake

Makes about **IO** servings

3 tablespoons bread crumbs

3 cups cake flour

I 1/2 teaspoons baking powder

1/2 teaspoon salt

6 large eggs

9 tablespoons DaVero or other good-quality olive oil

3/4 cup firmly packed dark brown sugar

3/4 cup granulated sugar

Grated peel from 3 lemons

I 1/2 cups store-bought apple butter

Cinnamon Cream (page 174)

An eclectic group of about 100 people gathered to harvest olives at DaVero Olive Oil orchard in Sonoma County, California. Our picking was motivated not just by the sunny yet crisp autumn day and the constant conversation but also by the one rule of the day set forth by the owners, Ridge and Colleen. No food and wine were to be served until the last olive was picked. Seeing the tables set up on the wraparound porch, laden with bread and aluminum buckets filled with chilled wine, inspired us to strip the trees bare in record time. For the family-style lunch, Loretta Keller, owner of Bizou Restaurant in San Francisco, prepared braised rabbit with pumpkin sage sauce in the brick oven. The dessert buffet was a myriad of sweet offerings. I brought a cake I had created that incorporated DaVero's fruity olive oil. The Italians have been making olive oil cake for centuries. My recipe adds apple butter to give it an extra dimension, perfect for fall.

Preheat the oven to 350 degrees F. Grease a 10-inch Bundt pan and coat it with the bread crumbs.

Sift together the cake flour, baking powder, and salt.

In a large bowl, whisk together the eggs, olive oil, brown sugar, granulated sugar, and lemon peel. Stir in the apple butter. Stir in the dry ingredients until smooth.

Spread the batter into the prepared pan and bake until a skewer inserted in the middle comes out clean, about 50 minutes. Let the cake cool for 20 minutes at room temperature. Place a large plate over the pan and invert plate and pan together. Lift the pan off the cake. Let cool completely before slicing.

TO SERVE: Slice the cake thinly and serve with the Cinnamon Cream.

PLANNING AHEAD: The cake can be made a day in advance; wrap in plastic wrap and store at room temperature.

autumn "summer" pudding

Makes **8** servings

This recipe results from my determination to extend summer pudding into another season. The concept for the two is identical; I have just altered the fruit, as summer's bounty of berries is no longer available. Apples and pears are cooked until soft and then pureed. The apples are cooked for a while before adding the pears, since apples take longer to soften and release their juices. The salt and lemon juice enhance the flavor of the puree. These fall fruits have lower acidity than berries, so without the lemon juice and salt, the pudding would taste bland. Layers of brioche are soaked with the puree. Refrigerated and weighted down for several hours, a delicious, custardless pudding is created. Serve with crème fraîche as opposed to whipped cream—it has a tangy flavor that complements the pudding well.

Twenty-four 1 $\frac{1}{4}$-inch-thick slices brioche or other rich dense bread

6 medium apples (about 3 pounds), such as Jonathan Black, Fuji, or Braeburn

1 cup sugar

$\frac{1}{8}$ teaspoon salt

3 teaspoons freshly squeezed lemon juice

6 ripe pears (about 3 pounds), such as D'Anjou, Comice, or French Butter

1 $\frac{1}{4}$ cups apple cider or apple juice

Caramel Sauce (page 173)

Crème fraîche (store-bought or homemade, see page 172)

Cut each slice of brioche into 2-inch circles. (Save the scraps for bread pudding or bread crumbs.)

Peel, core, and slice the apples $\frac{1}{8}$ inch thick. Cook the apples, sugar, salt, and 2 teaspoons lemon juice in a large sauté pan over medium-high heat until the apples give off some liquid and begin to soften, about 5 minutes.

While the apples are cooking, peel, core, and slice the pears $\frac{1}{4}$ inch thick. Add the pears to the pan and continue to cook until the pears and apples are soft. Puree the mixture in a food processor or pass through a food mill.

Place the puree in a medium saucepan and stir in the apple cider and remaining 1 teaspoon lemon juice. Cook the puree over medium heat until warm.

Spoon 1 tablespoon of the puree into the bottom of each of eight 4-ounce ramekins. Using a pair of tongs, two forks, or your fingers, dip a circle of brioche into the puree, completely saturating it. Place the brioche in the bottom of the ramekin. Cover with 2 tablespoons of the puree. Repeat this layering process of soaked cake and puree until there are 4 pieces of brioche in each ramekin, ending with a tablespoon of puree.

Place the ramekins on a baking sheet and cover them with a piece of plastic wrap. Place another baking sheet on top and weight down with a heavy pot or canned goods. Make sure there is enough weight to compress the bread. Refrigerate for at least 6 hours to overnight.

TO SERVE: Run a knife along the inside edge of each ramekin, invert them onto dessert plates, and remove the ramekins. Spoon any puree that sticks to the bottom of the ramekin onto the top of the pudding. Warm the caramel sauce in a double boiler or microwave. Dollop some crème fraîche on top and drizzle some caramel around the plate.

PLANNING AHEAD: The pudding can be made up to 2 days in advance and kept refrigerated in the ramekins. Unmold just before serving.

8 ounces (1 cup) mascarpone
1 tablespoon plus 1 teaspoon good-quality honey
2 teaspoons sugar
Pinch of salt
3 tablespoons heavy (whipping) cream
Eight 4-inch prebaked tartlet shells (page 170)
1 1/2 pints raspberries
1/2 cup Raspberry Sauce (page 174)

raspberry–honey cream tartlets

Makes **8** servings

Fortunately, the raspberry season extends into fall. Delicate in taste as well as texture, dissolving in your mouth in a perfumed bouquet, raspberries are the preeminent berries. Aficionados will pay any price for great raspberries. Try to buy your raspberries at a farm stand near where they are grown. The small-scale raspberry growers I have met take great pride in their berries and will not sell anything that is not in top condition. You will never see mold on farm stand raspberries. When possible, buy organic raspberries. If they are free of pesticides, you will not have to wash them. Water diminishes the flavor and texture of the berries. Just inspect for bugs and brush off any dirt specks. | The quintessential way to present perfect raspberries is in a fresh tart. Cooking them would be blasphemous. Raspberries need little embellishment besides a buttery crust and some lightened cream. It is a good idea to make individual tarts so that each person can hoard their own.

In a medium bowl, whisk together the mascarpone, honey, sugar, salt, and cream until thick. Spread the mascarpone mixture in the bottom of each of the prebaked tartlet shells.

In a medium bowl, gently mix together the raspberries and 1/4 cup of the raspberry sauce.

TO SERVE: Place the raspberries on top of the filled tartlets. Place the tartlets on individual dessert plates and drizzle a little of the Raspberry Sauce around each. Serve immediately.

PLANNING AHEAD: The honey cream can be mixed a day in advance and kept refrigerated. Assemble the tarts right before you serve them.

apple splits

Makes **6** servings

6 small or 3 large apples (see headnote)
I ounce (2 tablespoons) unsalted butter
3 cups (750 ml bottle) sparkling apple cider
4 ounces dried apricots, cut into 3/8-inch pieces
$^{I}/_{4}$ cup golden raisins
$^{I}/_{4}$ cup sour cherries
I tablespoon dark rum
Caramel Sauce (page 173)
Vanilla Crème Anglaise (page 175)
Cinnamon Ice Cream (page 180)
I ounce ($^{I}/_{4}$ cup) pecan pieces, toasted (see page 26)
I ounce ($^{I}/_{4}$ cup) sliced almonds, toasted (see page 26)

As teenagers, my sister and I loved making banana splits for our two brothers. They were our guinea pigs for some first-class, some bizarre, and some truly awful flavor combinations. We would slice the bananas, scoop out several kinds of ice cream, layer sauces, and garnish with colorful toppings. I never was as big a fan of eating the dessert as I was of making it, even those few variations our brothers rated as successful. It wasn't until years later that I made a split I liked to eat as well as to prepare. | Throughout the world, there are thousands of types of apples, but you will usually never find more than a dozen available in your area. Even in the United States, where fruit is shipped all over the country, there are some apples that can only be found in certain regions. It is the regional apples that have the best taste. Learn what is available in your area and experiment to see which types are good for baking, sautéing, or pureeing. For this recipe, where the apple is baked, you must select a type that will be soft when cooked but will also hold its shape. I like to use Fuji, Winesap, or Jonathan. Apples should be stored in the refrigerator so they stay fresh and crisp longer.

Preheat the oven to 350 degrees F.

Halve the apples and core them. Place the apples in a single layer in a baking dish, cut-side up. (If they won't stay upright, slice a thin piece off the bottom of each apple.) Place 1 teaspoon of butter in the middle of each apple. Pour $^3/4$ cup of the apple cider over the apples. Cover the dish with aluminum foil. Bake the apples until a small sharp knife easily pierces the flesh and they still retain their shape, about 30 minutes.

While the apples are cooking, warm the remaining cider, the apricots, the raisins, and the sour cherries in a medium saucepan over medium heat until the fruit is soft, about 8 minutes. With a slotted spoon, remove the fruit, placing it in a small bowl. Increase to high heat and reduce the cider to $^1/2$ cup, about 5 minutes. Remove the pan from the heat and stir in the rum.

Warm the Caramel Sauce in a double boiler or in a microwave.

TO SERVE: Place 2 small halves or one large half of a baked apple on each of 6 dessert plates. Spoon some cider sauce and some Vanilla Crème Anglaise around the apples. Place a scoop of Cinnamon Ice Cream on top of each apple and sprinkle some softened dried fruit, pecans, and almonds over and around the apples. Drizzle the Caramel Sauce over the ice cream. Serve immediately.

PLANNING AHEAD: The apples can be baked a day in advance, kept refrigerated, and reheated in a preheated 350 degree F oven for 15 minutes. The cider sauce can be made a day ahead, kept refrigerated, and reheated in a double boiler or in a microwave.

cinnamon apple crêpes

Makes **6** servings

CRÊPE FILLING

    6 ounces (12 tablespoons) unsalted butter, softened

    $1/4$ cup sugar

    Grated peel of 1 orange

    Pinch of salt

    1 tablespoon apple brandy

    12 crêpes (page 169)

APPLE COMPOTE

    5 apples (about 2 pounds), such as Jonagold, Fuji, or Braeburn

    3/4 cup apple juice

    $1/2$ cup sugar

    $1/2$ cup water

    $1/2$ vanilla bean, split lengthwise

SAUCE

    $1 1/2$ teaspoons lemon juice

    1 tablespoon apple brandy

    Pinch of salt

    2 ounces (4 tablespoons) unsalted butter

    1 ounce ($1/4$ cup) pecan pieces, toasted (see page 26)

You can create a party or an entire menu around the arrival of a season's fruits or a specific dessert. When I create a dessert, I don't just put it on the table without some sort of story about the dessert's evolution or some historical tidbits on the showcased fruit—it would seem anticlimactic. For the arrival of apple season, I created this nontraditional way to enjoy the season's bounty. Decorate the table with different varieties of apples. You can serve hard apple cider (or sparkling to nondrinkers) as an aperitif. As a conversational tidbit you might share that, despite popular opinion, Johnny Appleseed did not scatter apple seeds across the eastern and midwestern parts of the United States. Rather, he developed nurseries that sold seedlings. (Apple trees do not grow readily from seed.)

TO MAKE THE FILLING: Mix together the butter, sugar, orange peel, salt, and brandy in a small bowl. Spread some of the butter mixture on 1 side of each of the crêpes. Fold each crêpe into quarters and place them in a single layer on a baking sheet. Cover with aluminum foil.

TO MAKE THE COMPOTE: Peel the apples. Using a melon baller, scoop out balls from the apple flesh. Be careful not to scoop into the core. Make 48 balls in total.

    In a medium-sized saucepan, bring the apple juice, sugar, water, and vanilla bean to a boil over medium-high heat. Boil until the sugar dissolves, about 30 seconds, then reduce the heat to medium. Place the apple balls in the apple syrup and cover them with parchment paper or aluminum foil. Poach the balls until they are soft but retain their shape, about 10 minutes, depending on the variety of apple being used. To test for doneness, pierce a ball with a paring knife. The knife should easily enter the fruit. Using a slotted spoon, place the apples in a bowl. Discard the vanilla bean but reserve the poaching liquid.

TO PREPARE THE CRÊPES: Preheat the oven to 350 degrees F. Heat the crêpes in the oven until warmed through, about 5 minutes.

    While the crêpes are in the oven, prepare the sauce: Heat the apple poaching liquid with the lemon juice, brandy, and salt in a large sauté pan over high heat until reduced by about one-third. Add the butter and apple balls and cook until the sauce thickens slightly.

TO SERVE: Place 2 crêpes on each of 6 dessert plates. Spoon some of the apple balls and sauce over the crêpes, then sprinkle with pecans. Serve immediately.

PLANNING AHEAD: The crêpe batter can be made several days in advance and kept refrigerated. The crêpes can be made and filled a day in advance and kept refrigerated. The apples can be poached a day in advance and kept refrigerated in the poaching liquid. Heat the crêpes and make the sauce right before serving.

Blitz Puff Pastry (page 168)
4 fresh plums (about 1 pound; see headnote)
1 1/2 tablespoons sugar
1 egg, lightly beaten
Orange Cream Sauce (page 175)

french plum tart

Makes **8** servings

French and Italian plums come at the end of summer and beginning of autumn, when other varieties have already disappeared. These plums are dark skinned with a yellow-brown flesh. They have a higher sugar content than earlier types and are more suitable for drying into prunes. Used fresh they are quite different from their dried counterpart. Simply sprinkling a little sugar on top, cooking them inside puff pastry, and serving the tart slightly warm is the best way to bring out their flavor. If your grocery store carries good-quality puff pastry, by all means purchase it but be sure it is made with butter. In a pinch I have gone into bakeries that sell baked puff pastry items and asked for a piece of it unbaked. Most bakeries are willing to oblige as long as you give them a little notice so they can have it on hand. | This recipe can be used as a base for any fruit tart. Adjust the sugar as necessary. Cook apples and pears before putting them in the tart. Berries and stone fruit can be put in as is.

Using a sharp knife, cut the dough into 2 pieces: one, two-thirds of the dough, the other, one-third. Refrigerate or freeze the smaller piece for another use. Divide the remaining dough into 2 pieces, one slightly bigger than the other. Return the smaller piece to the refrigerator. Lightly flour a work surface and place the larger puff pastry on the flour. Lightly flour the top of the puff pastry and roll into a 16-by-6-inch rectangle. Line the bottom and sides of a 14-by-4-inch rectangular tart pan with the dough.

Cut the plums into thirds and place them in the tart, completely covering the bottom. Sprinkle the sugar over them.

Place the smaller piece of puff pastry on a lightly floured work surface. Sprinkle the top with flour and roll into a 14-by-4-inch rectangle. Brush the tops of the edges of the plum-filled tart shell with the beaten egg. Place the top of the dough over the fruit-filled tart, pressing it into place. Brush the top with some of the beaten egg. Using a small sharp knife, diagonally mark the top of the dough in 1-inch intervals. Do not cut through the dough, just score it. Refrigerate the tart for at least 30 minutes or for several hours.

Preheat the oven to 375 degrees F. Place the tart pan on a baking sheet and bake until very golden brown, at least 45 minutes. Let cool for 10 minutes. Loosen the edges of the tart from the pan using a small sharp knife and remove from the pan.

TO SERVE: Place the tart on a rectangular platter. Serve slightly warm or at room temperature with the Orange Cream Sauce.

PLANNING AHEAD: The tart is best eaten the day it is made. Leftovers can be kept at room temperature and reheated.

individual german chocolate cakes

Makes **6** servings

Many classic desserts appear repeatedly in cookbooks and on dessert menus, but no two are made exactly alike. A dessert like German Chocolate Cake should have all the elements of the traditional recipe—chocolate, coconut, pecans, and a brown sugar topping—and should not stray too far from the original intent. Even when following this rule, another pastry chef's rendition of this favorite will not be the same as mine: it depends on the proportions of the ingredients. Too thick a layer of chocolate cake will make the dessert dry; too much cream will make it too pudding-like and overwhelm the chocolate taste. In this variation for German Chocolate Cake, I have stayed true to the classic but have made it more elegant by creating individual cakes.

COCONUT PASTRY CREAM

1 1/2 cups milk

1 1/4 cups unsweetened coconut, toasted (see page 24)

4 large egg yolks

1/4 cup sugar

Pinch of salt

1/4 cup all-purpose flour

CARAMEL PECAN SAUCE

3 ounces (6 tablespoons) unsalted butter

3 tablespoons granulated sugar

1/2 cup firmly packed dark brown sugar

3/4 cup heavy (whipping) cream

6 ounces (1 1/2 cups) pecan pieces, toasted (see page 26)

Indispensable Chocolate Cake, baked in an 8-inch square pan (page 176)

TO MAKE THE PASTRY CREAM: Warm the milk in a medium saucepan over medium heat, stirring occasionally, until hot, about 5 minutes. Turn off the heat and stir in the coconut. Cover the pan with plastic wrap and let steep for 10 minutes.

Strain the milk into a bowl, discard the coconut, and return the milk to the saucepan. Cook the coconut milk over medium heat, until hot and bubbling around the edges, about 1 minute.

Whisk the egg yolks, sugar, and salt in a medium bowl until blended. Whisk in the flour. Slowly whisk the coconut milk into the eggs. Place the mixture back into the saucepan. Cook over low heat, stirring continuously with a wooden or heat-resistant rubber spatula until thick, about 5 minutes. Whisk until smooth. Pour into a medium bowl and place plastic wrap directly on the surface of the cream. Refrigerate for at least 1 hour.

TO MAKE THE SAUCE: Melt the butter over medium heat in a small saucepan. Add the sugars and whisk until smooth. Whisk in the cream and bring to a boil over medium heat. Boil, stirring occasionally, until it bubbles and thickens slightly, about 8 minutes. Remove the sauce from the heat. Stir in the pecans.

TO ASSEMBLE THE CAKES: Run a knife around the inside edge of the chocolate cake pan. Place a cutting board on top of the pan. Invert the cake and pan together and remove the pan. Carefully peel off the parchment paper. With a serrated knife, trim the edges of the cake to form nine 2 1/4-inch squares. Cut each square in half horizontally, making 18 pieces total.

Place a piece of cake on each of 6 dessert plates. Spread about 1 1/2 tablespoons of the Coconut Pastry Cream over each of the cake pieces. Layer a second piece of cake on top and again cover with pastry cream. Place a third piece of cake on top. Pour warm Caramel Pecan Sauce over the tops. Serve immediately.

PLANNING AHEAD: The chocolate cake can be made a day in advance; wrap well in plastic wrap and store at room temperature. The Coconut Pastry Cream and the Pecan Caramel Sauce can both be made up to 2 days in advance and kept refrigerated. Reheat the sauce briefly in a microwave or double boiler. Assemble the cakes just before serving.

orange marmalade tart

Makes **8** servings

When I was a child, there was always a jar of marmalade in the cupboard. My parents had it on their toast every weekend, but I never liked it. (My preference was cinnamon sugar.) But with the years come wisdom, and I have come to recognize that good marmalade is much more than orange jam. Both the pulp and the skins of Seville oranges are cooked slowly for a long time, which softens the fruit and eliminates bitterness. The result is a spread with a complex flavor and a thick consistency. Seville oranges are often combined with lemons, sweet oranges, and sometimes limes or even kumquats or quince to make marmalade. | A good marmalade shouldn't be as sweet as jam. This is especially important for this tart, or it will be too cloying. I like Wilkin Marmalade, manufactured—like most good marmalades—in England. This is a recipe with very few ingredients. If you have rolled pastry in the freezer, it can be thrown together in no time.

$^1/_4$ cup sugar

2 large eggs

1 $^1/_2$ cups orange marmalade

$^1/_4$ cup heavy (whipping) cream

One 9-inch prebaked tart crust (page 170)

Preheat the oven to 350 degrees F.

In a medium bowl, whisk together the sugar and eggs until blended. Stir in the marmalade and cream. Spread into the prebaked tart shell. Bake until the tart is set, about 40 minutes. It will still be slightly wiggly in the center. Let cool to room temperature before serving.

PLANNING AHEAD: This tart should be made and served the same day.

triple-layer pear brioche sandwiches

Makes **8** servings

COOKED PEAR SLICES

6 ripe pears (Comice, French Butter, or d'Anjou)

3 tablespoons sugar

1 teaspoon freshly squeezed lemon juice

Pinch of salt

24 slices brioche or other rich dense bread ($1/2$ inch thick)

4 ounces (8 tablespoons) unsalted butter, softened

$1/2$ teaspoon ground cinnamon

$1/4$ cup sugar

Crème fraîche (store-bought or homemade, see page 172)

When sautéing pears, choose a large sauté pan—you want as much surface area as possible so the slices are in a single layer. If they are sitting on top of each other in a smaller pan, they will stew and you will end up with pear sauce instead of pear slices. (If you do not have a large sauté pan, cook the pears in batches.) Slice them about $1/2$ inch thick and cook them on a high enough heat so the juices can evaporate. If the juices are still thin and watery when the pears finish cooking, remove the pears from the pan and reduce the liquid until it is slightly syrupy. Stir the pears back into the juice. The reduced juice will greatly enhance the pears' flavor. Conversely, if the pears are not ripe enough, they will remain dry when cooked and you will need to add some pear or apple juice and some butter to the pan to compensate.

TO PREPARE THE PEARS: Peel, halve, and core the pears, and slice them $1/2$ inch thick. Place the slices in a large sauté pan with the sugar, lemon juice, and salt and cook over medium-high heat until they are soft but still retain their shape (see head-note). Remove the pear slices from the pan. Increase to high heat and reduce any juices until syrupy. Reserve the syrup. Let the pears cool to room temperature.

Preheat the broiler.

Cut each brioche slice into a 2-inch circle using a round cutter or drinking glass. Mix together the butter, cinnamon, and sugar. Place the brioche circles on a baking sheet. Put under the broiler and toast until golden brown. Turn the circles over and spread the cinnamon-sugar butter on the untoasted side. Broil until golden brown.

TO SERVE: Place 1 piece of toasted brioche, cinnamon-sugar-side up, on each of 8 dessert plates. Spoon some cooked pears on top. Put a small dollop of crème fraîche over the pears. Repeat with another layer of brioche, pears, and crème fraîche. Top with a third brioche toast. Drizzle some of the pear syrup around each brioche sandwich. Serve immediately.

PLANNING AHEAD: The pears and the syrup can be made a day or two in advance; store in the refrigerator and let them come to room temperature before serving. If the syrup is still too thick to pour, microwave briefly to reheat. Broil the brioche and layer the sandwiches just before serving.

grandmother's apple cake

Makes **8** servings

5 tablespoons plus $\frac{1}{4}$ cup sugar

1 cup all-purpose flour

$\frac{1}{2}$ teaspoon salt

1 teaspoon baking powder

1 large egg

2 tablespoons milk

1 teaspoon vanilla extract

2 ounces (4 tablespoons) unsalted butter, softened

2 medium Golden Delicious apples (about 1 pound, 3 ounces)

$\frac{1}{2}$ teaspoon cinnamon

Chantilly Cream (page 172)

Many baking novices feel that you can't become an accomplished baker unless you learned at your grandmother's knee. They assume every pastry chef got started in childhood getting secret tips as Granny (or Nona, Gremmy, or Nana), with flour on her apron, patiently demonstrated how to roll a pie crust and then fill it with freshly picked apples from an orchard two feet from the back door. Granted, this is a good way to become a baker but it is not the only way. Let's face it—many of our grandmothers did not bake and this means we are on our own. While both of my grandmothers were wonderful women from whom I learned a great deal, their baking repertoires were limited (although my maternal grandmother made the absolute best chocolate frosting, which I still make to this day). | Don't use not having a baking grandmother as an excuse—it is never too late to start. To learn how to bake, with or without a grandmother, read everything you can get your hands on and bake, bake, and then bake some more. This straightforward recipe, from my husband's Grandmother Sue, is great for beginners. Just follow the instructions, take your time, and have fun.

Preheat the oven to 400 degrees F. Coat the bottom of a 10-inch cast-iron skillet with cooking oil spray. Sprinkle 2 tablespoons of the sugar over the bottom of the pan.

Sift together the flour, salt, and baking powder. In a small bowl, whisk together the egg, milk, and vanilla.

In another bowl, mix together the butter and the $\frac{1}{4}$ cup of sugar until light, 1 minute with a stand mixer or 2 minutes with a handheld mixer. By hand, stir in one-third of the flour mixture and then one-third of the milk mixture just until mixed. Add the remaining flour and milk in 2 additions.

Spread the batter in the skillet. It will be thick and a little sticky. If difficult to spread, wet the back of a spoon or ends of your fingers to push the batter out to the edges.

Peel and core the apples. Cut them in slices $\frac{1}{8}$ inch thick. Starting from the outer edge of the cake, arrange the apples in concentric circles, slightly overlapping, over the top of the batter, completely covering it. In a small bowl, mix together the remaining 3 tablespoons sugar with the cinnamon and sprinkle it over the apples.

Bake until a skewer inserted in the middle comes out clean, 20 to 25 minutes. Let cool for 10 minutes. Loosen the edges and bottom of the cake from the pan using a large metal spatula. Place a large plate on top of the cake. Invert the pan and plate together, then remove the pan. Place another plate on top of the cake and invert it again so it is right-side up.

Serve with Chantilly Cream.

PLANNING AHEAD: This cake is best warm out of the oven. It can be made a day in advance; wrap in plastic wrap and store at room temperature. Reheat in a preheated 350 degree F oven for 10 minutes.

orange pound cake

WITH CONCORD GRAPE COMPOTE

Makes **6** servings

The Concord grape season is short and even then they can be difficult to find, so keep your eyes peeled. The powdery coating often seen on grapes is not bad—it is an indicator that the grapes are fresh. We are all familiar with Concord grapes in jelly, but the potential for their pairing goes far beyond humble pb&j. As with berries, the simplest and quickest preparation is best. | To prepare the grapes for the compote, cut them in half with a serrated knife to avoid crushing them. Pick out the seeds with a toothpick or the end of a paring knife. Sauté briefly to soften the skins, warm them through, and bring out their fragrance. The grapes should not disintegrate or lose their shape.

POUND CAKE

1 3/4 cups all-purpose flour

1 1/2 teaspoons baking powder

1/2 teaspoon salt

6 ounces (12 tablespoons) unsalted butter, softened

1 2/3 cups sugar

Grated peel of 2 oranges

4 large eggs

3/4 cup sour cream

GRAPE COMPOTE

1/4 cup sugar

1/2 cup water

1 pound Concord grapes, halved and seeded

1/2 ounce (1 tablespoon) unsalted butter

Chantilly Cream (page 172) or Cinnamon Cream (page 174)

Preheat the oven to 350 degrees F. Butter and flour a 9-by-5-by-3-inch loaf pan.

TO MAKE THE POUND CAKE: Sift together the flour, baking powder, and salt.

Using an electric mixer, beat the butter, sugar, and orange peel on medium-high speed until light and fluffy, about 2 minutes with a stand mixer or 4 minutes with a handheld mixer. Add the eggs one at a time, beating well after each addition. On low speed, stir in the sour cream and then the dry ingredients.

Spread the batter into the prepared pan. Bake until a skewer inserted in the middle comes out clean, about 60 minutes.

Let the cake cool in the pan for 15 minutes. Run a small knife along the inside edge of the pan to loosen it. Invert the cake onto a wire rack and remove the pan. Let cool completely.

TO MAKE THE COMPOTE AND SERVE THE CAKE: Slice the pound cake about 1 1/2 inches thick. Cut each slice in half diagonally. Place 2 pieces on each of 6 dessert plates so they are at an angle. In a large sauté pan, cook the sugar and water over medium-high heat until the mixture comes to a boil. Add the grapes and the butter. Cook until the grapes give off a little juice and are warmed through, about 1 minute. With a slotted spoon, spoon the grapes over the cake slices. Continue to cook the sauce until it starts to thicken slightly, about 2 minutes longer. Pour some sauce on the grapes and around the cake. Dollop some Chantilly Cream or Cinnamon Cream on top. Serve immediately.

PLANNING AHEAD: The pound cake can be made a day ahead; wrap in plastic wrap and store at room temperature. The grape compote should be made just before serving.

persimmon rum mousse

WITH CRÈME FRAÎCHE AND CARAMEL SAUCE

Makes **6** servings

Every year, the gusty fall winds blow away the leaves on the persimmon tree outside my mother-in-law's office, leaving the plump orange-red fruit hanging like ornaments. It is a curious sight but at the same time reassuring. I know winter has not completely descended as long as there are still fresh persimmons to pick. | For baking, I prefer the acorn-shaped Hachiya persimmons. They are extremely astringent when unripe but if allowed to soften, become sweet and make a wonderful puree. Do not confuse Hachiya persimmons with Fuyu persimmons: a Fuyu resembles a flat-topped tomato, is delicious eaten hard, and is often used in salads.

2 teaspoons powdered gelatin

2 tablespoons water

$^1/_4$ cup granulated sugar

$^1/_4$ cup dark rum

2 tablespoons freshly squeezed orange juice

4 large egg yolks

I cup persimmon puree (see sidebar)

2 tablespoons firmly packed brown sugar

$^1/_2$ teaspoon ground ginger

I cup heavy (whipping) cream

Caramel Sauce (page 173)

Crème fraîche (store-bought or homemade, see page 172)

Line six 4-ounce tomato paste cans (see headnote on page 44) with parchment or wax paper. Place the cans on a baking sheet lined with parchment or waxed paper.

Fill a medium saucepan one-third full of water and heat the water until very hot. Place the gelatin in a small heat-resistant bowl and stir in the 2 tablespoons of water. Let sit until the gelatin has dissolved, about 5 minutes. Carefully place the bowl in the pan of hot water and melt the gelatin, about 2 minutes. Remove from the pan and set aside.

Bring the pan of water to a boil. In a large stainless-steel bowl, whisk together the granulated sugar, rum, orange juice, and egg yolks until blended. Place the bowl over the pan of boiling water, making sure the water does not touch the bottom of the bowl. Whisk the mixture vigorously until thick, tripled in volume, and no longer foamy, about 2 minutes. Remove the bowl from the heat. Whisk in the softened gelatin. Whisk in the persimmon puree, brown sugar, and ginger.

In a large bowl, whip the cream until soft peaks form. Fold the cream into the persimmon mixture. Place the mousse in a large measuring cup with a lip and pour into the prepared tomato paste cans. Refrigerate until set, at least 3 hours.

TO SERVE: Warm the Caramel Sauce in a double boiler or microwave and drizzle some on each of 6 dessert plates. Using a metal spatula, transfer a persimmon mousse onto each plate. Lift the cans off and carefully peel off the parchment paper. Spoon some crème fraîche on top of each mousse and serve.

PLANNING AHEAD: The persimmon mousses can be made a day in advance and kept refrigerated.

For overnight ripening of Hachiyas, place them in the freezer and in the morning let them thaw on a countertop. Once defrosted, they will be soft and ready to use. To make puree, cut out the green tops and puree the persimmons in a food processor. Strain through a medium-mesh sieve to eliminate any skins. One persimmon will make about $^1/_2$ cup of puree. The puree can be frozen.

pear–caramel swirl ice cream

WITH PECAN COOKIES

Makes **6** servings

In the realm of pastry arts, the pear is underappreciated. It does not have the popularity of the apple even though it has more to offer. Pears have a wonderful perfume and complex flavor. An apple is intense and upfront in its flavor. A pear is more subtle and sophisticated. In baking, almost anything you can do with apples you can make with pears with more delicious results. The main reason for its low esteem is that the pear is one of the few fruits that must ripen after it is picked. When purchased, pears are generally hard and must sit on the countertop for two to three days before they soften and are ready to be consumed. Using pears in desserts must be premeditated, but they are worth all the planning. Take the trouble to think ahead and purchase pears in advance—you will be rewarded.

PEAR–CARAMEL SWIRL ICE CREAM

6 large ripe pears (about 3 pounds)
1 1/3 cups sugar
1 tablespoon freshly squeezed lemon juice
1/2 cup pear liqueur
6 large egg yolks
1/8 teaspoon salt
2 cups milk
2 1/2 cups heavy (whipping) cream
1 cup cold Caramel Sauce (page 173)

PECAN COOKIES

3 1/2 ounces (7 tablespoons) unsalted butter, softened
1/3 cup sugar
1/2 teaspoon vanilla extract
1/2 cup plus 2 tablespoons all-purpose flour
Pinch of salt
1 ounce (1/4 cup) pecan pieces, toasted (see page 26)

TO MAKE THE ICE CREAM: Peel, halve, and core the pears. Slice them 1/2 inch thick. Cook the pear slices, 1/3 cup of the sugar, the lemon juice, and 2 tablespoons of the pear liqueur over medium-high heat in a large sauté pan until the pears are soft and the juices have evaporated, 10 to 15 minutes, depending on how juicy the pears are. Stir occasionally in the beginning and more frequently once the juices begin to evaporate. Let cool for 10 minutes and then puree in a food processor or through a food mill. Refrigerate until cold.

In a large bowl, whisk together the egg yolks, salt, and 1/2 cup of the sugar.

Cook the milk, cream, and remaining 1/2 cup sugar in a medium saucepan over medium-high heat, stirring occasionally, until hot and bubbling around the edges, 8 to 10 minutes. Slowly whisk the cream mixture into the eggs. Pour the liquid back into the pan. Cook over medium-low heat, stirring continuously, until the cream coats the back of a metal spoon, about 5 minutes. Strain and cool over an ice bath (see page 28). Refrigerate for at least 2 hours.

Stir together the pear puree, the cream mixture, and the remaining 6 tablespoons pear liqueur. Freeze in an ice cream maker according to the manufacturer's instructions. Immediately after removing the ice cream from the machine, with one or two motions, fold the Caramel Sauce into the ice cream, creating a swirled pattern. Do not completely mix the ice cream and the Caramel Sauce together—there should be large streaks of caramel. Freeze until hard, about 2 hours.

CONTINUED

TO MAKE THE COOKIES: Using an electric mixer, beat the butter, sugar, and vanilla until smooth, about 30 seconds with a stand mixer or 1 minute with a handheld mixer. On low speed, add the flour, salt, and pecans. Between pieces of wax paper, roll the cookie dough into a 9 1/2-by-1 1/4-inch log. Refrigerate the log until hard, at least 1 hour.

Preheat the oven to 350 degrees F. Line 2 baking sheets with parchment paper.

Slice the log into cookies 1/8 inch thick. Place on the prepared baking sheets 1 inch apart. Bake until golden brown, 12 to 15 minutes. Let cool on the baking sheets.

TO SERVE: Place 2 scoops of ice cream in individual bowls with several cookies.

PLANNING AHEAD: The ice cream can be made several days in advance. The cookie dough can be made several days in advance and kept refrigerated or frozen. Bake the cookies the day you plan to serve them.

It is important to cook all the watery liquid out of the pears to maximize their flavor and, more importantly, to prevent the ice cream from being icy.

figamaroles

Makes about **24** 3-inch cookies

COOKIE DOUGH

3 large hard-boiled egg yolks

6 ounces (12 tablespoons) unsalted butter, softened

Grated peel from 1 lemon

$^1/_2$ teaspoon vanilla extract

6 tablespoons sugar

1 $^1/_2$ cups all-purpose flour

Pinch of salt

FIG FILLING

8 ounces (1 $^1/_2$ cups) dried figs

$^3/_4$ cup freshly squeezed orange juice

$^3/_4$ cup water

The idea for this dessert came when I was playing tennis and missed a backhand shot. In frustration I exclaimed, "Oh figamarole!" Now I don't know about you, but that word is not a part of my vocabulary or in any dictionary of the English language that I inspected. I looked at my partner and said, "That would be a great name for a dessert!" Obviously it would have to have figs in it and it should be rolled...

TO MAKE THE COOKIE DOUGH: Place the egg yolks, butter, lemon peel, vanilla, and sugar in a food processor and process until smooth. Add the flour and salt and again process until smooth. Wrap the dough in plastic wrap and refrigerate for at least 1 hour to overnight.

While the dough chills, make the filling: Cut the figs into quarters, discarding the stems. Put the figs, orange juice, and water in a medium saucepan and bring to a boil over medium-high heat. Simmer until the figs are soft, about 5 minutes. Drain the figs, discarding the liquid. Let cool to room temperature, then puree the figs in a food processor.

Preheat the oven to 350 degrees F. Line a baking sheet with parchment paper.

On a lightly floured work surface, roll half of the dough (keep the remaining dough refrigerated) into a rectangle $^1/_8$ inch thick. Cut the dough into 3-inch squares. Place 1 teaspoon of the fig puree along one end of a square. Pick up the edge of the dough with a metal spatula and roll the dough around the filling. Place the roll, seam-side down, on the prepared baking sheet. Roll the rest of the cookies in the same manner. Scraps of dough can be rerolled. The dough gets soft quickly. If it gets difficult to roll, refrigerate for 15 minutes.

Bake the figamaroles until golden brown, about 12 minutes.

PLANNING AHEAD: The figamaroles can be formed a day ahead and kept refrigerated. They are best baked and eaten the same day.

pumpkin upside-down cake

WITH CRANBERRY PECAN TOPPING

Makes **8** to **10** servings

Creating desserts with pumpkin is always a challenge. Pumpkin puree is so strong and thick that practically everything you make with it ends up tasting like pumpkin pie. And although pumpkin pie will always be a favorite dessert, especially for Thanksgiving, it is nice to be able to offer an alternative. The recipe for this cake comes from a very good home cook, Bea Petcavich. I transformed it into an upside-down cake with cranberries and pecans in a brown sugar topping. It's a festive cake for autumn—don't wait until November to try it!

8 ounces (16 tablespoons) unsalted butter
1 cup firmly packed brown sugar
2 cups cranberries
4 ounces (1 cup) coarsely chopped pecans, toasted (see page 26)
2 large eggs
1 cup pumpkin puree
6 tablespoons vegetable oil
1 1/2 cups all-purpose flour
1 cup granulated sugar
1 1/2 teaspoons baking powder
1 teaspoon cinnamon
1/4 teaspoon salt
Chantilly Cream (page 172)

Preheat the oven to 350 degrees F. Line the bottom of a 9-inch square pan with parchment paper.

Melt the butter in a small saucepan over medium heat. Add the brown sugar and whisk until smooth. Pour the brown sugar mixture into the bottom of the prepared pan.

In a medium bowl, combine the cranberries and pecans. Place them in the pan over the brown sugar mixture.

In a large bowl, whisk together the eggs, pumpkin puree, and oil. In another bowl, sift together the flour, granulated sugar, baking powder, cinnamon, and salt. Stir the flour mixture into the pumpkin mixture. Carefully spread the batter over the cranberry pecan topping.

Bake the cake until a skewer inserted in the middle comes out clean, 35 to 40 minutes. Let cool for 10 minutes on a wire rack. Place a large plate or platter on top of the cake. Invert the cake and plate together, then remove the pan. Carefully peel off the parchment paper.

Let cool completely before serving. Serve with Chantilly Cream.

PLANNING AHEAD: The cake can be made a day in advance; wrap in plastic wrap and store at room temperature.

pumpkin zuccotto

Makes **8** to **10** servings

Italy has more wonderful desserts than just the ubiquitous biscotti and tiramisu we have all grown so fond of. When in Italy, I search out pasticcerìas for traditional regional desserts. One such dessert, popular mostly in Florence but also in other parts of Italy, is zuccotto. Cake, flavored creams, and chocolate are layered in a bowl, refrigerated for several hours, and then inverted and unmolded. The resulting dome shape is said to resemble Il Duomo, the famous cathedral in Florence. | Since *zucca* is the Italian word for "pumpkin," I incorporated pumpkin into my adaptation of this dish. I thought it appropriate that its flavor match its name. This dessert doesn't need any sauces and garnishes. It is fantastic as is.

PUMPKIN CAKE

6 ounces (12 tablespoons) unsalted butter, softened

1 1/2 cups sugar

3 large eggs

3/4 cup pumpkin puree

1 3/4 cups all-purpose flour

1/4 teaspoon salt

1 1/2 teaspoons baking powder

1/2 teaspoon cinnamon

1/4 teaspoon ground ginger

1/8 teaspoon nutmeg

1/2 cup milk

1/2 teaspoon vanilla extract

CREAM FILLING

2 cups heavy (whipping) cream

1/4 cup sugar

1 teaspoon vanilla extract

1 tablespoon dark rum

1 cup mini chocolate chips

Preheat the oven to 350 degrees F. Grease and line the bottom of a 9-by-13-inch baking pan with parchment paper.

TO MAKE THE CAKE: Beat the butter and sugar with an electric mixer on medium speed until light and fluffy, 1 minute with a stand mixer or 2 to 3 minutes with a handheld mixer. Add the eggs, one at a time, mixing well and scraping down the sides of the bowl after each addition. On low speed, mix in the pumpkin puree.

In a medium bowl, sift together the flour, salt, baking powder, cinnamon, ginger, and nutmeg. In a small bowl, combine the milk and vanilla. On low speed, in two additions, alternately stir the flour and the milk mixtures into the egg mixture.

Spread the batter evenly into the prepared pan. Bake until a skewer inserted in the middle comes out clean, about 30 minutes. Let cool completely.

TO MAKE THE CREAM FILLING: Whip the cream, sugar, and vanilla until stiff but not grainy. Fold in the rum and mini chocolate chips.

Grease and line a 2-quart bowl with plastic wrap. Run a knife around the inside edge of the cake pan and then invert the pan onto a cutting board. Remove the pan and carefully peel off the parchment paper. Cut the pumpkin cake into quarters and cut each quarter in half horizontally. Cut a cake piece to fit the bottom of the bowl and place it in the bowl. Cut about 8 pieces of cake, each about 4 by 2 inches, and place them side by side vertically against the sides of the bowl with the short ends touching the cake circle. There will be a triangular gap between each of the rectangles. Cut and fit cake pieces to fill the gaps. The bowl should be completely covered with cake pieces.

Spoon half of the cream into the bowl. Cover the top of the cream with cake pieces. Press the cake down gently. Spread the remaining cream on top and cover with the remaining cake pieces. Press the cake down again. If necessary, trim the vertical ends of the pieces so they are even with the edge of the bowl. Refrigerate until serving, at least 2 hours.

TO SERVE: Place a large plate on top of the zuccotto and invert the bowl and plate. Remove the bowl and carefully peel off the plastic wrap. Cut with a serrated knife into wedges.

PLANNING AHEAD: The zuccotto can be made a day in advance and kept refrigerated, well wrapped in plastic wrap.

fig galettes

WITH CINNAMON MARSALA SABAYON

Makes **6** servings

In the United States, we don't know from figs, unless you are talking about Fig Newtons. Those familiar only with dry figs do not know how much fresh figs have to offer. Figs come in black and green varieties. The most common (and my favorite) is the Black Mission fig. It has a beautiful dark purple color, a quintessential fig shape, and a sweet taste with a smooth texture. Figs are not subtle in their flavor and shouldn't be served with flavors that they can dominate. When I was creating this rather sophisticated dessert, the individual components—the semolina galette, the poached figs, and the cinnamon Marsala sabayon—were all delicious, but something was missing. I presented it to my husband, explaining that it wasn't quite right: the dessert needed one additional subtle element but I had no idea what that might be. He suggested toasted pistachios sprinkled over the top and he was right. It was just what was needed to enhance the other flavors and bring them together into a finished dessert.

GALETTES

$^1/_2$ cup semolina

$^1/_2$ cup all-purpose flour

2 tablespoons sugar

Grated peel from 1 orange

1 teaspoon baking powder

Pinch of salt

1 $^1/_2$ ounces (3 tablespoons) cold unsalted butter

$^1/_3$ cup heavy (whipping) cream

CINNAMON MARSALA SABAYON

4 large egg yolks

5 tablespoons sugar

Pinch of salt

$^1/_4$ cup Marsala

2 tablespoons sherry

$^3/_4$ cup heavy (whipping) cream

$^1/_8$ teaspoon cinnamon

FIGS

$^1/_2$ cup sugar

1 cup orange juice

24 fresh Black Mission figs

1 ounce (3 tablespoons) finely chopped pistachios, toasted, for garnish (see page 26)

TO MAKE THE GALETTES USING A FOOD PROCESSOR: Put the semolina, flour, sugar, orange peel, baking powder, salt, and butter in a food processor. Pulse the flour mixture until the butter is pea sized. This will happen very quickly, so be careful not to overprocess. With the machine running, pour the cream into the food processor. Process just until the dough comes together.

TO MAKE THE GALETTES USING A STAND MIXER: Put the semolina, flour, sugar, orange peel, baking powder, salt, and butter in the bowl of an electric mixer. On low speed, using the paddle attachment, mix in the butter until it is pea sized. Pour the cream into the flour mixture and stir until the dough comes together.

Form the dough into a 5-inch disk and wrap in plastic wrap. Refrigerate until firm, at least 1 hour to overnight.

Line a baking sheet with parchment paper. On a lightly floured work surface, roll the dough out $^1/_8$ inch thick. If the dough is hard and difficult to roll, let it sit at room temperature to soften slightly, 10 to 15 minutes. Cut the dough into six 5-inch circles. Using a metal spatula, place the circles in a single layer, $^1/_2$ inch apart, on the prepared baking sheet. Refrigerate the circles for at least 30 minutes or up to several days.

CONTINUED

Preheat the oven to 350 degrees F. With the tines of a fork, pierce the top of each galette about 20 times. Bake until light gold in color, about 15 minutes.

TO MAKE THE SABAYON: In a large stainless-steel mixing bowl, whisk together the egg yolks, sugar, and salt until blended. Whisk in the Marsala and sherry. Place the bowl over a pan of simmering water, making sure the bottom of the bowl does not touch the water. Whisk vigorously until thick, about 3 minutes. Remove the bowl from the pan and place it over an ice bath (see page 28). Let cool to room temperature, whisking occasionally.

In a medium bowl, combine the cream and the cinnamon. Whip until soft peaks form. Fold the cream into the cooled Marsala mixture. Refrigerate until ready to serve the galettes.

TO PREPARE THE FIGS: Preheat the oven to 400 degrees F. Stir together the sugar and orange juice in an ovenproof baking dish large enough to hold the figs in a single layer. Add the figs and coat them with the liquid. Bake until plump and soft, about 15 minutes.

Using a slotted spoon, place the figs in a single layer on a plate to cool. Pour the poaching liquid into a small saucepan. Reduce the liquid over high heat until it thickens slightly, about 3 minutes. Let cool to room temperature.

TO SERVE: Place a galette on each of 6 dessert plates. Spoon about 2 table-spoons of sabayon on top of the galettes, leaving 1/2 inch around the edge of each galette exposed. Cut the stems off the figs and cut the figs in half. Place some figs in the middle of each galette. Drizzle the reduced poaching syrup over and around the figs. Sprinkle with toasted pistachios and serve immediately.

PLANNING AHEAD: The galette dough can be made and rolled several days in advance; wrap well in plastic wrap and refrigerate. Bake and serve the galettes the same day. The sabayon can be made a day in advance and kept refrigerated. The figs can be baked several hours in advance and kept at room temperature.

Double boilers are good for melting ingredients, but for whisking sabayons I prefer a makeshift double boiler: place a stainless-steel bowl filled with the ingredients over a pan of simmering water. The rounded bottom of the bowl allows for smooth whisking and prevents the eggs from getting stuck in the corner and scrambling.

ricotta cheesecake

WITH DRIED CHERRIES AND GOLDEN RAISINS

Makes **10** servings

Graham crackers make an ideal crumb crust for cheesecakes and pies and complement practically all fillings. While I will make my own graham crackers for the Banana Cream–Graham Cracker Napoleons (page 134), for a crumb crust I won't bother. | I am a big fan of dense, New York–style cheesecakes but sometimes I am in the mood for a cheesecake recipe like the following that is not quite as heavy. Using ricotta and folding in whipped egg whites lightens the cake. Drain off any liquid from the ricotta before adding it. Putting dried fruit on top of the crust and not adding them to the batter, keeps the filling smooth and creamy, just as a cheesecake should be.

CRUST AND FRUIT MIXTURE

5 ounces (1 cellophane package) graham crackers

2 1/2 ounces (5 tablespoons) unsalted butter, melted

3/4 cup dried sour cherries

3/4 cup golden raisins

1/4 cup dark rum

3/4 cup water

RICOTTA FILLING

4 large eggs, separated

1/2 cup plus 2 tablespoons sugar

4 cups ricotta cheese

1/2 cup heavy (whipping) cream

5 tablespoons flour

Grated peel of 1 lemon

Grated peel of 1 orange

1/2 teaspoon vanilla extract

Preheat the oven to 350 degrees F.

TO MAKE THE CRUST AND FRUIT MIXTURE: In a food processor, finely grind the graham crackers. Place the crumbs in a bowl and stir in the melted butter. Press the crumbs in the bottom of a 9-inch springform pan. Bake until golden brown, about 8 minutes. Cool to room temperature.

Place the sour cherries, raisins, rum, and water in a medium saucepan and bring to a boil. Cook over medium-high heat, stirring occasionally, until the liquid evaporates, about 10 minutes. Cool slightly and then sprinkle the fruit over the graham cracker crust.

TO MAKE THE FILLING: Using an electric mixer on medium-high speed, whip the egg yolks and the 1/2 cup sugar until light in color, 1 minute with a stand mixer or 2 minutes with a handheld mixer. Reduce to low speed, add the ricotta and cream, and mix until blended. Stir in the flour, lemon and orange peels, and vanilla.

In a separate bowl, whip the egg whites with an electric mixer until soft peaks form. While still mixing, add the remaining 2 tablespoons sugar in a steady stream. Whip until smooth and satiny, 1 minute with a stand mixer or 3 minutes with a handheld mixer. Fold the egg whites into the batter in two additions.

Spread the batter over the prepared crust. Bake until a skewer inserted in the middle comes out clean, about 50 minutes.

Let the cake cool at room temperature on a wire rack for 15 minutes. Run a knife around the inside edge of the cake pan to remove the cheesecake from the sides of the pan and help eliminate cracking as it continues to cool. Refrigerate until completely cold, at least 6 hours, before serving. Slice with a hot dry knife (see page 29).

PLANNING AHEAD: The cheesecake can be made a day ahead and kept refrigerated.

walnut cake

WITH CHOCOLATE ORANGE SABAYON
AND VANILLA CRÈME ANGLAISE

Makes **8** servings

Setting up the lunch table under the cool shade of a walnut tree seemed like a good idea until my guests and I heard the first sound of something hit the ground behind us on the patio. We paid no attention as we were distracted by the aroma of the tagliatelle with porcini mushrooms that my husband was placing on the table. Then three walnuts fell on the middle of the table. We left them there as our centerpiece as we enjoyed lunch under this gentle bombardment. Then two walnuts fell into one friend's lap. By this point we had finished the pasta and decided to start collecting the intruders, rather than sit still and risk getting hit on the head. In no time we had gathered quite a few nuts, discovering many that had already fallen and were hidden in the grass. We cracked some open and enjoyed them with figs from a neighboring tree. They were exquisite, fresh without a trace of bitterness. Since we had to crack the shells open to uncover the nuts, each morsel was greatly appreciated. I then made dessert using our leftover walnuts, borrowing the following cake recipe from my friend Nadia.

WALNUT CAKE

10 ounces (2 1/2 cups) walnuts, toasted (see page 26)

1 cup sugar

6 large eggs, separated

2 tablespoons potato flour

1 teaspoon baking powder

1 tablespoon instant espresso or coffee powder

1/4 teaspoon salt

1/8 teaspoon cream of tartar

CHOCOLATE ORANGE SABAYON

4 large egg yolks

1/4 cup sugar

Pinch of salt

1/3 cup freshly squeezed orange juice

1 1/2 ounces bittersweet chocolate, finely chopped

3/4 cup heavy (whipping) cream

Vanilla Crème Anglaise (page 175)

Preheat the oven to 350 degrees F. Butter the sides and bottom of a 9-inch spring-form pan and line the bottom with parchment paper.

TO MAKE THE CAKE: In a food processor, finely grind the walnuts with 1/4 cup of the sugar.

With an electric mixer on medium speed, whip the egg yolks and remaining 3/4 cup sugar in a large bowl until light in color and tripled in volume, 2 minutes with a stand mixer or 4 minutes with a handheld mixer.

On low speed, stir in the walnuts, potato flour, baking powder, espresso, and salt.

With an electric mixer on medium-high speed, whip the egg whites and cream of tartar until soft peaks form, 1 minute with a stand mixer or 3 minutes with a handheld mixer. Fold the egg whites into the walnut batter in three additions.

Spread the batter into the prepared pan and bake until a skewer inserted in the middle comes out clean, 35 to 40 minutes. Let cool completely. Remove the cake from the pan by running a knife along the inside edge, releasing the latch, and inverting the cake onto a large plate. Remove the pan bottom and the parchment paper.

TO MAKE THE SABAYON: In a large stainless-steel mixing bowl, whisk together the egg yolks, sugar, and salt until blended. Whisk in the orange juice. Place the bowl over a large saucepan of simmering water, making sure the bowl does not touch the water (see sidebar on page 126). Whisk vigorously until thick, about 3 minutes. Remove the bowl from the pan. Whisk in the chocolate. Place the bowl over an ice bath (see page 28). Let cool to room temperature, whisking occasionally.

CONTINUED

Whip the cream until soft peaks form. Fold the cream into the cooled chocolate mixture and refrigerate until ready to serve.

TO SERVE: Spoon some crème anglaise onto each of 8 dessert plates. Slice 8 pieces of cake and place them on the plates. Spoon chocolate orange sabayon on top.

PLANNING AHEAD: The walnut cake can be made a day in advance; wrap well in plastic wrap and store at room temperature. The sabayon can be made a day in advance and kept refrigerated.

BAKED QUINCE

3 large quince

3/4 cup sugar

1 cup water

1 cup Sauvignon Blanc

2-inch cinnamon stick

1/2 vanilla bean, split lengthwise and seeds removed

WALNUT SHORTCAKES

3 ounces (3/4 cup) walnuts, toasted (see page 26) and finely ground

3 tablespoons sugar

1 3/4 cups all-purpose flour

2 1/2 teaspoons baking powder

1/2 teaspoon salt

3 ounces (6 tablespoons) cold unsalted butter

1/2 cup heavy (whipping) cream

Chantilly Cream (page 172)

walnut shortcakes

WITH BAKED QUINCE

Makes **6** servings

To many Americans, *quince* is a word in an English novel having to do with tea and scones on the lawn. The English are proud defenders of this yellow, bumpy, pear-shaped fruit and heap quince preserves on their scones. Perhaps it is due to my English heritage, but I am a big fan of quince as well. Do not be put off by the fruit's unripe characteristics—it is pale, tough, bitter, and dry, hardly tantalizing to the palate. But cook it gently in the oven for a couple of hours, and you will transform it into a beautiful, brownish red fruit with a delicious, complex flavor. Quince must be paired with richly flavored ingredients such as walnuts. This combination of walnut shortcake, cream, and baked quince creates an earthy and striking dessert perfect for autumn.

TO MAKE THE QUINCE: Preheat the oven to 325 degrees F. Peel, quarter, and core the quince and place in a single layer in an ovenproof baking dish. Heat the sugar, water, wine, cinnamon stick, and vanilla bean in a small saucepan over medium-high heat until it comes to a boil. Pour the hot syrup over the quince. Cover the baking dish with aluminum foil and bake until a knife easily pierces the flesh, 2 to 2 1/2 hours. With a slotted spoon, remove the quince from the pan. Cut the quince into 1-inch pieces. Put the poaching liquid in a small saucepan. Over medium-high heat, reduce the liquid until slightly syrupy, about 5 minutes. Place the syrup and the quince pieces in a medium bowl. Cool to room temperature and refrigerate.

TO MAKE THE SHORTCAKES: Preheat the oven to 350 degrees F. Line a baking sheet with parchment paper. Combine the walnuts, sugar, flour, baking powder, and salt in a large bowl. Using a pastry blender, the paddle attachment on an electric stand mixer, or 2 knives, mix in the butter until it is pea sized. Add the cream and stir until the dough comes together. Form the dough into a 5-inch disk. On a lightly floured work surface, pat or roll the dough out to 3/4 inch thick. Cut into 2 1/2-inch circles. Place the circles on the prepared baking sheet, several inches apart, and bake until golden brown, about 25 minutes.

TO ASSEMBLE THE SHORTCAKES: Preheat the oven to 325 degrees F. Cut each shortcake in half horizontally. Reheat the quince for 10 minutes and the shortcakes for 5 minutes. Place the bottom of a shortcake on each of 6 dessert plates. Place some quince and some syrup over and around the shortcakes. Top with some Chantilly Cream. Place the top halves of the shortcakes over the cream. Drizzle the remaining sauce around the shortcakes. Serve immediately.

PLANNING AHEAD: Shortcakes are best made the day they are to be eaten. The quince can be prepared several days in advance and kept refrigerated.

WINTER DESSERTS   In winter I feel especially fortunate to make my living as a pastry chef. Being in the kitchen all day, kept snug by the ovens, makes me feel content and grounded.

Of all the seasons, winter has fewer fresh ingredients, so pastry chefs must be resourceful in creating desserts. Chocolate, nuts, citrus, and bananas are the main staples during this time of year. I dabble with chocolate during other months, but winter is where it really belongs. It can be an accent flavor, as in the Chestnut Chocolate Marquise (page 149), or get top billing, as in the Triple Chocolate Trifles (page 161).

In winter, if the weather cannot keep us warm, then our desserts must. Tropical fruits brighten up the grays of the season. Howling winds, chipping ice off the sidewalk, and numb toes can be faced head-on when you know there is a delicious dessert waiting for you inside. Enjoying Bittersweet Chocolate Fondue (page 135) with your sweetheart in front of a crackling fire keeps you from dreaming about summer or warmer temperatures.

Holidays bring us together for treasured times during these months, and desserts are a large part of our traditions, whether making truffles as gifts or a special creation for Hanukkah or Christmas Day.

134 banana cream–graham cracker napoleons

135 bittersweet chocolate fondue

137 apple caramel bread pudding

138 hot buttered rum and banana compote with vanilla bean ice cream

139 bittersweet chocolate mousse cake with white chocolate sauce

141 lemon mousse with citrus compote

143 chocolate mocha truffles

144 chocolate–peanut butter truffles

146 citrus cake

149 chestnut chocolate marquise

151 raspberry ice cream sandwiches

155 macaroon pineapple napoleons

156 frozen maple cream–pecan pie

157 double chocolate hot chocolate

158 hazelnut sandwich cookies

160 meyer lemon buttermilk tart

161 triple chocolate trifles

163 espresso cupcakes with milk chocolate ganache and white chocolate frosting

165 rum caramel–marinated oranges over vanilla bean ice cream

banana cream–graham cracker napoleons

Makes **6** servings

Traditionally, a napoleon consisted of puff pastry and sweetened pastry cream, but now the term is used more widely to refer to something layered, either sweet or savory. Any cookie, wafer, or pastry that is crispy and light works well in a dessert napoleon. It must be strong enough to hold the layers of cream but light enough that you can easily break it with your utensil. The pleasure of eating a napoleon is as much about texture as it is about taste. For this reason it is important not to assemble napoleons ahead of time, or they will get soggy. Here, homemade graham crackers, vanilla cream, and bananas create a napoleon version of a banana cream pie. Tossing the bananas in a splash of rum gives the dessert a little zip. Use just the lime and orange juices if you want to omit the alcohol.

GRAHAM CRACKERS

4 ounces (8 tablespoons) unsalted butter, softened

1/4 cup firmly packed brown sugar

3 tablespoons granulated sugar

2 teaspoons honey

1/4 teaspoon vanilla extract

I cup all-purpose flour

1/2 cup whole wheat flour

1/8 teaspoon salt

1/4 teaspoon baking soda

1/2 teaspoon cinnamon

4 to 5 medium bananas, cut into 1/4-inch slices

I teaspoon freshly squeezed lime juice

I teaspoon freshly squeezed orange juice

I teaspoon dark rum

Chantilly Cream (page 172)

TO MAKE THE GRAHAM CRACKERS: Using an electric mixer on medium-high speed, beat together the butter, brown sugar, 2 tablespoons of the granulated sugar, the honey, and the vanilla until smooth and creamy, 30 seconds with a stand mixer or 1 minute with a handheld mixer.

Sift together the flours, salt, baking soda, and 1/4 teaspoon of the cinnamon and add to the butter mixture, mixing on low speed until the dough comes together. Form the dough into a 5-inch disk and wrap in plastic wrap. Refrigerate for 1 hour to overnight.

Preheat the oven to 350 degrees F. Line 2 baking sheets with parchment paper. If the dough is too hard to roll, let it sit at room temperature to soften slightly, 15 to 30 minutes. Roll the dough out to 1/16 inch thick. Trim into a 12-by-15-inch rectangle. Cut into twenty 3-inch squares. Place them on the prepared baking sheets. Make small holes in the top of the squares with the tines of a fork.

In a small bowl, mix together the remaining 1 tablespoon granulated sugar and 1/4 teaspoon cinnamon. Sprinkle the cinnamon sugar over the graham crackers. Bake until nicely browned, about 8 minutes. Let the graham crackers cool to room temperature on the baking sheets. Store in an airtight container.

TO SERVE THE NAPOLEONS: Gently mix together the bananas, lime and orange juices, and the rum. Place a graham cracker on each of 6 dessert plates. Place some bananas and Chantilly Cream on each graham cracker. Continue layering in the same manner, ending with a third graham cracker.

PLANNING AHEAD: The graham cracker dough can be made and rolled 2 days ahead and kept refrigerated. To ensure crispness, bake the graham crackers the day they are to be served. Slice the bananas just before serving.

bittersweet chocolate fondue

Makes **8** servings

As part of the entertaining process, I love to go to the grocery store. Most people view this as an inconvenience or hassle, but I look at is as a prelude to the party. I like to wander down the aisles, thinking about my guests—who I will introduce to whom, which friend I haven't seen in a long time. As I push my cart by the dairy case, I think about how my cousin always likes extra whipped cream on his dessert. As I put the chocolate in my cart, I remember to buy extra to ensure that there will be enough for my husband to nibble on for an afternoon snack. I go down an aisle even if I don't think I need anything in it. You never know what you will discover. The candy aisle can be a great inspiration for new desserts, either conceptually or as an added ingredient. At the frozen food case, I see if there are any new ice cream flavors I need to try. This dessert is perfect for grocery store browsing. The treats you can dip into chocolate fondue are limited only by your own imagination. I have included my favorites, but be sure to wander the aisles of your grocery store and see what additions you come up with.

FONDUE

$^1/_2$ cup heavy (whipping) cream

$^1/_2$ cup milk

11 ounces bittersweet chocolate, finely chopped

POSSIBILITIES FOR DIPPING (ALLOW AT LEAST 6 ITEMS PER PERSON)

Small ice cream balls coated in cookie crumbs

Marshmallows

Biscotti

Graham crackers

Banana chunks

Almonds

Caramels

Mini profiteroles

Angel food cake cubes

Pound cake cubes

Pretzels

Mini coconut macaroons

TO MAKE THE FONDUE: Warm the cream and milk in a medium saucepan over medium heat until hot and bubbling around the edges, about 5 minutes. Remove from the heat. Add the chopped chocolate, let sit for 30 seconds, and then whisk until smooth. Pour the chocolate into 2 small decorative bowls.

Place the bowls on the table along with a platter of items to be dipped. Serve with long forks to make dipping easier.

PLANNING AHEAD: The fondue can be made a day in advance and kept refrigerated. Reheat in a microwave or double boiler.

apple caramel
bread pudding

Makes **8** servings

I created this dessert for Christmas Eve dinner. In this busiest of seasons with all the last-minute shopping and visiting that occurs, I like to serve a comforting and delicious dessert that can be made in stages over the course of several days. The apples, custard, and bread can be prepared up to two days before you bake the pudding, which itself can be baked a day in advance. When Christmas Eve finally arrives, the dessert is finished, and I can relax, toast the holiday with a glass of sparkling wine, and enjoy being with my family. | This is sometimes called "bread-and-butter pudding" because the bread slices are buttered before the custard is poured over them. I omit the buttering step, as my variation is tasty enough without the butter. I use Golden Delicious apples—no genetic relation and a much superior apple to the Red Delicious. When sautéed, they become soft but the slices retain their shape. Choose a sweet baguette over a sourdough one for a more neutral taste.

4 Golden Delicious apples (about 1 3/4 pounds)

1 ounce (2 tablespoons) unsalted butter

1/3 cup apple juice

2 teaspoons freshly squeezed lemon juice

Scant 1 cup sugar

8 ounces sweet baguette, crust on, cut into 3/4-inch pieces
     (about 4 1/2 cups)

1/2 cup water

1 1/2 cups heavy (whipping) cream

3 cups milk

4 large eggs

5 large egg yolks

1/4 teaspoon salt

1/4 teaspoon cinnamon

1/4 teaspoon ground ginger

Preheat the oven to 350 degrees F. Peel, core, and slice the apples 1/4 inch thick.

Cook the apple slices, butter, apple and lemon juices, and 1/4 cup of the sugar in a large sauté pan over medium-high heat until the apples are soft, about 15 minutes.

Evenly spread the apple slices into the bottom of a 2 1/2-quart ovenproof baking dish. Place the bread pieces on top of the apples.

Stir together 2/3 cup of the sugar and the water in a medium saucepan and cook over medium heat until the sugar has dissolved, about 3 minutes. Increase to high heat and cook, without stirring, until the sugar is amber colored, 8 to 10 minutes. Remove from the heat. Wearing oven mitts, carefully stir about 1/2 cup of the cream into the caramel. Be careful, as the caramel will sputter when the cream is added. If it sputters violently, stop stirring. Let the bubbles subside and then stir again. Carefully stir in the remaining cream. Stir in the milk.

In a large bowl, whisk together the eggs, egg yolks, and salt. Whisk a quarter of the caramel cream into the eggs. Add the remaining caramel cream and whisk until incorporated. Pour the caramel cream into the pan over the apples and bread pieces. Using a metal spatula, gently press the bread pieces into the liquid, coating them.

Bake the bread pudding for 35 minutes. While it is baking, stir together the cinnamon, ginger, and the remaining 1 1/2 tablespoons sugar in a small bowl. After 35 minutes, sprinkle the sugar over the top of the bread pudding. Continue baking until the tips of the bread pieces are golden brown and a small knife inserted in the middle comes out coated with thickened custard, about 10 minutes. Serve warm.

PLANNING AHEAD: The bread pudding can be reheated. If you make it more than 3 hours in advance; refrigerate the pudding. Reheat in a preheated 325 degree F oven for 15 minutes.

hot buttered rum and banana compote

WITH VANILLA BEAN ICE CREAM

Makes **6** servings

Bananas come from a perennial herb plant, not a fruit tree. The stem of the plant, which can grow up to forty feet in a single year, is made up of thousands of overlapping, tightly stacked leaves. Clusters, or "hands," of bananas wrap around the stem. One banana plant can weigh up to a thousand pounds. This excessive weight causes the stem to bend and the bananas to point upward toward the sky, looking like they are growing upside down. A large red flower adorns the very top of the plant like a crown. Quite an exotic and grand habitat for a fruit we haphazardly slice over our morning cereal! | Historically, shipments of bananas from the tropics to Europe or the United States were often accompanied by another tropical specialty—dark rum. This combination is a natural not only for transport but also for flavor.

3/4 cup brown sugar

6 tablespoons dark rum

3/4 cup water

I tablespoon freshly squeezed lemon juice

1/8 teaspoon cinnamon

3 ounces (6 tablespoons) unsalted butter, softened

4 large bananas or 6 medium bananas, cut into I-inch diagonal slices

Vanilla Bean Ice Cream (page 179)

In a large sauté pan, cook the brown sugar, rum, water, lemon juice, and cinnamon over medium-high heat, stirring frequently, until the sugar dissolves and the liquid thickens slightly, about 4 minutes. Add the butter and bananas. Cook until the butter has melted and the bananas are warmed through, about 1 minute.

TO SERVE: Place a scoop of ice cream into each of 6 bowls. Spoon some sauce and bananas over it and serve immediately.

PLANNING AHEAD: The compote should be made just before serving.

bittersweet chocolate mousse cake

WITH WHITE CHOCOLATE SAUCE

Makes **10** to **12** servings

There is such a bewildering array of chocolate available in stores today that the only way to become educated about it, I concluded, is to try as many kinds as possible. I urge you to do likewise. You'll find that chocolate ranges in taste the way wine does. Some brands are smooth and subtle, while others are very intense, almost sharp. Some have a berry aroma; a few have coffee undertones. Invite a bunch of friends over for a chocolate tasting. Try to include Valrhona, Callebaut, Lindt, Ghirardelli, El Rey, Guittard, and Scharffen Berger. You should taste the chocolate by itself, and baked into chocolate desserts. (If your guests are willing, give them this recipe and have them each bring a cake made with one of the chocolate brands.) Compare the differences among them. You will find that each person will have a personal favorite; price does not necessarily dictate preference. Keep an open mind and an open palate. Where the beans were grown, how they are roasted, and the amounts of chocolate liquor and cocoa butter all influence the flavor of chocolate. The best part of a chocolate tasting is that, unlike a wine tasting, you can eat as much as you want and still drive home.

BITTERSWEET CHOCOLATE MOUSSE CAKE

- 2 cups finely ground chocolate cookie crumbs (Nabisco Famous Cocoa Wafers or chocolate biscotti crumbs)
- 3 ounces (6 tablespoons) unsalted butter, melted
- 15 ounces bittersweet chocolate, finely chopped
- 9 large egg yolks
- $1/2$ cup sugar
- Pinch of salt
- 6 tablespoons prepared coffee, cooled to room temperature
- 2 $1/2$ cups heavy (whipping) cream

WHITE CHOCOLATE SAUCE

- 8 ounces white chocolate, finely chopped
- $1/2$ cup water

TO MAKE THE MOUSSE CAKE: Stir the cookie crumbs together with the melted butter in a medium bowl. Press them in the bottom of a springform pan. Refrigerate for 30 minutes.

Melt the chocolate in a double boiler (see page 23). Stir until smooth. Remove from the heat.

Bring a medium saucepan one-third full of water to a boil. Whisk the egg yolks in a medium stainless-steel bowl with the sugar, salt, and coffee until combined. Set the bowl over the pan of boiling water, making sure the water does not touch the bottom of the bowl. Whisk vigorously until thick, 2 to 3 minutes. Remove the bowl from the heat and whisk in the melted chocolate. Cool the chocolate mixture, stirring occasionally with a rubber spatula, to room temperature.

Whip the cream until firm but still smooth peaks form. Fold one quarter of the cream into the chocolate mixture. After it is almost completely incorporated, fold in half of the remaining cream. Fold in the remaining cream. (Folding the chocolate cream into the cream in batches prevents the chocolate from getting too hard and creating chocolate chips.)

Spread the chocolate mousse over the crumbs in the springform pan. Refrigerate until set, at least 3 hours to overnight.

TO MAKE THE SAUCE: Melt the white chocolate together with the water in a double boiler (see page 23). Stir until smooth. Refrigerate the sauce until thick, at least 1 hour.

TO SERVE: Slice the mousse cake using a hot dry knife (see page 29). Serve the sauce in a pitcher alongside the cake.

PLANNING AHEAD: The mousse cake can be made a day or two in advance and kept refrigerated. The sauce can be made several days in advance and kept refrigerated. Let sit at room temperature for 30 minutes before serving.

LEMON MOUSSE

5 large eggs

$2/3$ cup granulated sugar

$2/3$ cup freshly squeezed lemon juice

$3/4$ cup heavy (whipping) cream

BRANDY SNAPS

2 ounces (4 tablespoons) unsalted butter

6 tablespoons firmly packed dark brown sugar

$1/4$ cup corn syrup

6 tablespoons all-purpose flour

2 teaspoons brandy

CITRUS COMPOTE

2 medium Ruby Red grapefruit

3 large blood oranges

3 large tangerines

1 vanilla bean

Granulated sugar, as needed

lemon mousse

WITH CITRUS COMPOTE

Makes **6** servings

Superb-tasting desserts don't have to be complicated, and simple desserts are not necessarily one-dimensional. In every dessert, there should be highs and lows for your palate. Here, the intense lemon cream provides the primary hit, but two varieties of oranges and Ruby Red grapefruit add subtle color and taste that are crucial to the dish. The vanilla supplies background flavor, while the brandy snaps offer a crunchy texture that sets off the creaminess of the mousse. After just one bite, you will pull the bowl in closer and glance around to see if anyone is going to take it away before you have had a chance to scrape it clean.

TO MAKE THE MOUSSE: In a medium bowl, whisk together the eggs, granulated sugar, and lemon juice until blended. In a small heavy-bottomed saucepan, cook the mixture over medium-low heat, stirring constantly with a flat heat-resistant or wooden spatula until thick, about 8 minutes.

Strain the mousse into a clean bowl. Place plastic wrap directly on the surface and refrigerate until cold, about 1 hour.

In a medium bowl, whip the cream to soft peaks. Fold in the cold lemon mousse. Refrigerate until ready to serve.

TO MAKE THE BRANDY SNAPS: Preheat the oven to 350 degrees F. Line 2 baking sheets with parchment paper.

Melt the butter with the brown sugar and corn syrup in a small saucepan over medium heat, stirring occasionally. Remove from the heat and stir in the flour and brandy.

On the prepared baking sheets, drop 1 teaspoon of the batter for each cookie, about $2^{1}/2$ inches apart. (The cookies will spread as they bake.) Bake until bubbling and golden brown, 8 to 10 minutes. Remove from the oven and let the cookies sit for 15 to 30 seconds. One at a time, remove each cookie from the baking sheets with a metal spatula and place it upside down on the countertop. Quickly wrap it around the handle of a wooden spoon and then slide it off the end. (If the cookies get too cool, they will break if you try to roll them. If this happens, place them back in the oven for a minute to warm them up. If they are too hot, they will fall apart when you pick them up.)

CONTINUED

TO MAKE THE CITRUS COMPOTE: With a sharp knife, cut the rind off the grapefruit, blood oranges, and tangerines. Over a medium bowl to catch any juices, separate the segments from the membrane using a paring knife. Put the segments into the bowl. As you finish each piece of fruit, squeeze any remaining juice out of the membrane into the bowl. Cut the vanilla bean in half lengthwise and scrape out the seeds. Place the seeds in the bowl with fruit. Reserve the bean for another use. Taste the juice. If it is too tart, add a couple teaspoons of sugar. Depending on the natural sweetness of the citrus, you may or may not need any sugar. Refrigerate until you are ready to serve.

TO SERVE: Place some citrus segments in the bottom of each of 6 bowls. Spoon some mousse over the top. Place 2 Brandy Snaps in the mousse. Serve immediately.

PLANNING AHEAD: The lemon mousse and the citrus segments can be made a day in advance and kept refrigerated. The Brandy Snaps can also be made a day in advance; store in an airtight container at room temperature.

chocolate mocha truffles

Makes **30** 1-inch truffles

Chocolate truffles may be petite, but their flavor is huge. Made of chocolate, cream, and flavorings, they deliver in one or two bites the fulfillment of a whole dessert. Coffee and peanut butter go well in truffles, because, like chocolate, they have bold flavors. Creating chocolate desserts for serious chocoholics can be tricky. Not enough chocolate in a dessert will make them sneer with disapproval at the wimpy taste. But too much chocolate in a dessert can actually crush the rich chocolate essence. Even chocolate lovers are mad for these truffles, which taste rich and decadent but are not intensely chocolaty.

3/4 cup heavy (whipping) cream
1 tablespoon ground coffee
6 ounces bittersweet chocolate, finely chopped
4 ounces milk chocolate, finely chopped
1/3 cup cocoa powder

Warm the cream in a small saucepan over medium-high heat, stirring frequently, until hot and bubbling around the edges, about 3 minutes. Remove the pan from the heat, add the coffee, and cover the pan. Let steep for 10 minutes.

Strain the cream into a bowl and discard the coffee. Return the cream to the pan. Again, heat the cream until it is bubbling around the edges. Remove the pan from the heat.

Put the two chocolates in a medium bowl and pour the cream over them. Let sit for 30 seconds, then whisk until smooth. Spread the chocolate cream in a 9-inch pan or pie plate. Refrigerate until hard, at least 1 hour to overnight.

Place the cocoa powder on a plate or in a pie dish. Line 2 baking sheets with parchment or wax paper.

Using a measuring teaspoon or melon baller, scoop out 30 heaping spoonfuls of the truffle mixture. Place them in a single layer on one of the prepared baking sheets. When all of the scoops have been made, lightly roll them between the palms of your hands to give them a nice round shape. If at any point the chocolate gets too warm, making the truffles difficult to roll, refrigerate the chocolate for 30 minutes until it firms up.

Roll the truffles, a few at a time, in the cocoa powder. Place in a single layer on the second baking sheet. Cover with plastic wrap and refrigerate.

Before serving the truffles, let them sit at room temperature to soften slightly, 15 to 30 minutes. This will make them a little creamier.

PLANNING AHEAD: The truffles can be made a week in advance and kept refrigerated.

To scoop truffles: Dip the spoon or melon baller in hot water after every couple of scoops. Tap gently on the sheet pan to loosen the truffle mixture. To keep your hands clean while rolling truffles, wear thin rubber gloves. This will also keep the truffles from getting too soft if your hands are too warm.

chocolate–
peanut butter
truffles

Makes **30** 1-inch truffles

Like their cousin, the Chocolate Mocha Truffle, these are quite sinful tasting, but the coffee is exchanged for peanut butter flavor.

$^{1}/_{2}$ cup heavy (whipping) cream

10 ounces bittersweet chocolate, finely chopped

$^{1}/_{4}$ cup smooth peanut butter

$^{1}/_{2}$ cup unsalted peanuts, ground

Warm the cream in a small saucepan over medium-high heat, stirring frequently, until hot and bubbling around the edges, about 3 minutes. Put the chocolate in a medium bowl and pour the cream over it. Let sit for 30 seconds, then whisk until smooth. Whisk in the peanut butter. Spread the chocolate cream in a 9-inch pan or pie plate. Refrigerate until hard, at least 1 hour to overnight.

Place the ground peanuts on a plate or in a pie dish. Line 2 baking sheets with parchment or wax paper.

Using a measuring teaspoon or melon baller, scoop out 30 heaping spoonfuls of the truffle mixture. Place them in a single layer on one of the prepared baking sheets. When all of the scoops have been made, lightly roll them between the palms of your hands to give them a nice round shape. If at any point the chocolate gets too warm, making the truffles difficult to roll, refrigerate the chocolate for 30 minutes until it firms up.

Roll the truffles, a few at a time, in the ground peanuts. You may need to gently press the peanuts into the truffles to get them to stick. Place in a single layer on the second baking sheet. Cover with plastic wrap and refrigerate.

Before serving the truffles, let them sit at room temperature to soften slightly, 15 to 30 minutes. This will make them a little creamier.

PLANNING AHEAD: The truffles can be made a week in advance and kept refrigerated.

citrus cake

Makes **10** to **12** servings

A visit to the produce section in winter shows an abundance of oranges, lemons, and limes. Start inspecting the signs more closely and you will discover numerous hybrids of these familiar fruits. It can be a little hard to keep them all straight but it's fun to experiment with them; they can be interchanged in many recipes using citrus. This recipe incorporates many different kinds of citrus for appearance and taste. For the zest in the cake, I like to use tangerines and Tahiti or Persian limes for their bright reddish orange and green colors, respectively. A tangerine is a type of mandarin. You could also use a tangelo, a cross between a tangerine and a grapefruit. A commonly seen tangelo is the Minneola. For the filling, I use a regular lemon rather than a Meyer lemon (a hybrid between an orange or mandarin and a lemon; see recipe introduction on page 160) because I want a puckery-tart curd. For the segments between the layers, I use Clementines or Satsumas, two more types of mandarins. These mandarin varieties can easily be sectioned with their membrane intact so the filling will not become runny. I like to use lime and lemon juices in the glaze to cut the sweetness and green, yellow, and orange zest for a confetti appearance.

CAKE

3 ounces (6 tablespoons) unsalted butter, softened

1 1/2 cups granulated sugar

Grated peel from 2 limes

Grated peel from 2 tangerines

2 1/4 cups cake flour

1 tablespoon baking powder

1/4 teaspoon salt

3/4 cup milk

3/4 teaspoon vanilla extract

1 1/2 tablespoons freshly squeezed tangerine juice

3 large eggs

LEMON CURD

3 large egg yolks

3 large eggs

3/4 cup granulated sugar

1/2 cup freshly squeezed lemon juice

Grated peel from 1 tangerine

1 1/2 ounces (3 tablespoons) unsalted butter

4 mandarin oranges, peeled and segmented (preferably Clementines or Satsumas)

CITRUS GLAZE

3 cups confectioners' sugar

1/4 cup freshly squeezed lemon juice

2 tablespoons freshly squeezed tangerine juice

Grated peel from 1 tangerine

Grated peel from 1 lemon

Grated peel from 1 lime

Preheat the oven to 350 degrees F. Grease and line three 9-inch cake pans with parchment paper.

TO MAKE THE CAKE: With an electric mixer on medium speed, beat together the butter, granulated sugar, and lime and tangerine peels until smooth, 2 minutes with a stand mixer or 4 minutes with a handheld mixer.

Sift together the flour, baking powder, and salt. In a small bowl or glass measuring cup, stir together the milk, vanilla, and tangerine juice.

On low speed, alternately add the dry ingredients and the milk to the butter mixture in 3 additions, stirring well after each addition. On medium speed, add the eggs one at a time, mixing well after each addition. Beat for 1 minute with a stand mixer or 3 minutes with a handheld mixer. Evenly divide the batter among the prepared cake pans.

Bake the cakes until a skewer inserted in the middle comes out clean, 15 to 20 minutes.

Let cool for 15 minutes. Unmold the cakes by running a knife around the inside edge of the pans. Place a large plate on top of each of the pans and invert pan and plate together. Remove the pans and carefully peel off the parchment paper. Let cool completely.

TO MAKE THE LEMON CURD: Whisk together the egg yolks, eggs, and granulated sugar. Whisk in the lemon juice. Cook in a double boiler, stirring constantly, until thickened, about 5 minutes. Remove the pan from the heat and stir in the tangerine peel and butter. Place the curd in a bowl and cover the surface with plastic wrap. Refrigerate until cold, at least 30 minutes.

Fold the mandarin segments into the curd.

TO MAKE THE GLAZE: Sift the confectioners' sugar into a bowl. Stir in the lemon and tangerine juices, and the tangerine, lemon, and lime peels. Whisk until smooth.

TO ASSEMBLE THE CAKE: Place 1 cake layer on a large cake plate or platter with a rim. Spread half of the curd over the cake. Place a second cake layer over the curd and spread the remaining curd on top. Place the third cake layer on top. Slowly pour the citrus glaze over the cake. Serve immediately.

PLANNING AHEAD: The cake can be made a day in advance; wrap in plastic wrap and store at room temperature. The curd can be made a day in advance and kept refrigerated. Make the glaze and assemble the cake the day you serve it. The cake can be assembled without the glaze several hours in advance and kept refrigerated. Thirty minutes before serving, remove the cake from the refrigerator. Pour the glaze on just before serving.

CHESTNUT FILLING

2 1/2 teaspoons powdered gelatin

5 tablespoons water

1 1/2 cups sugar

1 1/4 cups heavy (whipping) cream

2 cups sour cream

2 cups crème fraîche (store-bought or homemade, see page 172)

3/4 cup unsweetened chestnut puree

1/2 teaspoon vanilla extract

1/8 teaspoon salt

Grated peel from 1 orange

LADYFINGERS

3 tablespoons cake flour

2 tablespoons cornstarch

1 1/2 tablespoons cocoa powder

3 large eggs, separated

1/4 cup plus 1/3 cup sugar

Chocolate Sauce (page 173)

chestnut chocolate marquise

Makes **12** servings

Many pastry chefs do not like their recipes tinkered with. But as long as someone doesn't say a recipe is mine after they fiddle with it, I have no problem with changes. Having others adapt my recipes lets me look at them from a new angle. This recipe began as Chestnut Cream in my first book, *Stars Desserts*. A friend and fellow pastry chef, Janet Rikala, played with that recipe to make a charlotte using chocolate ladyfingers. She served it with a pear compote. Her addition of ladyfingers gave me the idea of making a marquise. I lightened up the filling and added grated orange peel. Feel free to transform this into something new.

TO MAKE THE FILLING: In a small glass measuring cup, mix together the gelatin and the water. Set aside to soften for 10 minutes.

Fill a medium saucepan one-third full of water and bring it to a boil. In a stainless-steel bowl, whisk together the sugar, cream, sour cream, crème fraîche, and chestnut puree. Set the bowl over the boiling water over medium heat and stir occasionally until the mixture is hot. The chestnut puree will break up as the mixture heats. Remove the bowl from the heat.

Turn off the heat under the pan and place the dish of gelatin in the hot water to dissolve the gelatin until translucent, about 3 minutes. (You may need to remove some of the water in the pan—it should not be higher than the measuring cup.)

Whisk the vanilla, salt, and orange peel into the chestnut mixture. Whisk in the dissolved gelatin. Refrigerate the chestnut cream, folding occasionally with a rubber spatula, until the mixture thickens but is still pourable, about 2 hours.

TO MAKE THE LADYFINGERS: Preheat the oven to 350 degrees F. With a pencil, draw lines, 3 inches apart, on 2 pieces of parchment paper as a guide for piping the ladyfingers. Line 2 baking sheets with the marked paper, pencil-side down. Fit a pastry bag with a 1/2-inch plain tip.

Sift together the cake flour, cornstarch, and cocoa powder.

With an electric mixer, whip together the egg yolks and 1/4 cup of the sugar on high speed until pale yellow and thick, 1 minute with a stand mixer or 2 minutes with a handheld mixer.

CONTINUED

In a separate bowl, whip the egg whites on high speed to soft peaks. In a steady stream add the remaining 1/3 cup sugar and whip until shiny and stiff, about 3 minutes with a stand mixer or 5 minutes with a handheld mixer.

Fold the sifted dry ingredients into the yolk mixture. Fold one-third of the whites into the cocoa mixture. When they are almost completely incorporated, fold in the remaining whites.

Place the batter into the prepared piping bag. Using the pencil markings as a guide, pipe ladyfingers out onto the prepared baking sheets, each 3 inches long and 3/4 inch wide, leaving 1/2 to 3/4 inch between them. Make at least 38 ladyfingers.

Bake the ladyfingers until they spring back lightly when touched on top, about 15 minutes. Let them cool on the baking sheets before removing them with a metal spatula.

Spray the inside of a 9-by-5-by-3-inch loaf pan with cooking oil spray and line with plastic wrap. Make sure to press the plastic wrap in the corners of the pan. With the pan positioned lengthwise in front of you, place 8 ladyfingers horizontally on the bottom of the pan. Place 4 ladyfingers standing up at both ends of the pan, tucking them between the edge of the pan and the ladyfingers on the bottom to make them stay up. Line the sides of the pan with ladyfingers in the same manner, using about 7 per side and tucking them between the sides and the ladyfingers on the bottom. If the last ladyfinger on each side is too wide, cut it to fit. Don't worry if the ladyfingers are taller than the pan.

When the chestnut filling is thick, but still pourable, carefully, without disturbing the ladyfingers, pour half of the filling into the prepared mold. With the pan positioned lengthwise in front of you, place 8 ladyfingers horizontally on top of the filling. Carefully pour the remaining chestnut filling into the pan. Refrigerate until set, 4 hours to overnight.

TO SERVE: Warm the chocolate sauce in a double boiler or microwave. Using a serrated knife, trim the end of the ladyfingers so they are even with the pan, cutting from the inside of the pan toward the outside. Invert a platter or large plate over the pan and invert the pan and plate together. Remove the pan and carefully peel off the plastic wrap. Slice the marquise and serve with Chocolate Sauce drizzled on each plate.

PLANNING AHEAD: The marquise can be made 2 days ahead and kept refrigerated. It takes a while to set, so it is a good idea to make it the day before you plan to serve it. The marquise can be unmolded several hours before serving.

raspberry ice cream sandwiches

Makes **8** sandwiches

I almost always prefer fresh over frozen ingredients, but two exceptions are filo dough and raspberries for puree. Using frozen filo dough is a thousand times easier than making it from scratch—it is one of those projects that is frankly too much of a hassle to bother with. (Although I made filo once just so I could say I did it.) | When making puree for sauce or in the following ice cream recipe, I prefer frozen raspberries over fresh. Fresh raspberries, although they taste fabulous, do not yield much liquid and can make a thin sauce. Frozen raspberries, defrosted and pureed, result in a thick puree with a good yield. Using frozen raspberries makes it possible to have a great-tasting raspberry dessert in the middle of winter. Feel free to cut these ice cream sandwiches smaller for a bite-size variation.

RASPBERRY ICE CREAM

12 ounces frozen raspberries (no sugar added), defrosted

4 large egg yolks

$^{1}/_{2}$ cup sugar

$^{1}/_{8}$ teaspoon salt

1 $^{1}/_{4}$ cups milk

1 $^{1}/_{4}$ cups heavy (whipping) cream

FILO RECTANGLES

2 ounces ($^{1}/_{2}$ cup) whole natural almonds, toasted (see page 26)

$^{1}/_{4}$ cup sugar

4 sheets filo (see page 25)

2 ounces (4 tablespoons) unsalted butter, melted

TO MAKE THE ICE CREAM: Puree the raspberries in a food processor or through a food mill. Strain the puree through a fine-mesh sieve to eliminate any seeds.

In a large bowl, whisk together the egg yolks, $^{1}/_{4}$ cup of the sugar, and the salt.

Warm the milk, the cream, and the remaining $^{1}/_{4}$ cup sugar in a saucepan over medium-high heat, stirring frequently, until hot and bubbling around the edges, about 5 minutes. Slowly whisk the liquid into the egg mixture. Return the milk and cream to the pan and cook over low heat, stirring constantly with a wooden spoon or rubber heat-resistant spatula, until it coats the back of a spoon, about 5 minutes. Strain through a medium-mesh sieve.

Cool over an ice bath (see page 28) and stir in the raspberry puree. Refrigerate until cold.

Freeze in an ice cream machine according to the manufacturer's instructions. While the ice cream is freezing, spray a 9-by-13-inch pan with cooking spray. Line the bottom and sides of the pan with a piece of plastic wrap. Spread the freshly churned ice cream into the pan and freeze until solid, 6 hours to overnight.

Place a piece of parchment paper on top of the pan. Place a cutting board on top of the parchment paper. Invert the pan and cutting board together. Remove the pan and then gently remove the plastic wrap. Cut the ice cream into rectangles 4 by 2$^{1}/_{2}$ inches. (Save scraps for nibbling.) Place the ice cream rectangles on a baking sheet in a single layer (or stack with plastic wrap between layers). Freeze until you are ready to serve the sandwiches.

CONTINUED

Preheat the oven to 375 degrees F. Line 2 baking sheets with parchment paper.

TO MAKE THE FILO RECTANGLES: Finely grind the almonds and the sugar together in a food processor. Put in a small bowl.

Lay the sheets of filo on a flat work surface. Remove 1 sheet from the stack and place it on the work surface in front of you. Cover the remaining sheets with a kitchen towel. Brush the single sheet with some of the melted butter and then sprinkle with one quarter of the almond sugar. Lay a second sheet of filo on top of the first and again butter and sugar it. Continue in the same manner with the remaining 2 sheets of filo.

Cut the filo stack into 16 rectangles, each 4 by 2 1/2 inches. Using a metal spatula, transfer the rectangles to the prepared baking sheets, placing them about 1/4 inch apart.

Bake the filo rectangles until golden brown, about 10 minutes. Let cool to room temperature.

TO SERVE: Place a rectangle of ice cream between 2 pieces of filo and serve immediately.

PLANNING AHEAD: The ice cream can be made and cut several days in advance. The filo should be baked and served the day it is made.

1 1/2 cups unsweetened shredded coconut, toasted (see page 24)

1/3 cup sugar

3/4 ounce (1 1/2 tablespoons) unsalted butter, melted and cooled

1 large egg

One medium pineapple (about 2 1/2-pounds), cut into 1/4-inch pieces (about 2 1/2 cups)

Chantilly Cream (page 172)

macaroon pineapple napoleons

Makes **6** servings

This coconut macaroon can assume many forms. As a part of Small Endings, the candy and confections plate at Farallon, they are three-dimensional domes, soft in the middle and crusty on the outside. In this dessert, they make an appearance as flat circles baked until crispy throughout. This versatile cookie recipe comes courtesy of Don Hall.

Preheat the oven to 350 degrees F. Butter 18 cupcake wells.

Stir together the coconut and sugar in a medium bowl, using a rubber spatula or wooden spoon. Stir in the melted butter and then the egg, and mix until combined.

Place 2 teaspoons of the coconut mixture into each of the cupcake wells. Using the back of a spoon dipped in water, press the coconut mixture into the well so it completely fills the bottom. Bake until golden brown, about 12 minutes. Let the macaroons cool in the pans. Using a small sharp knife or small offset spatula, loosen them from the wells and remove them.

TO SERVE: Place a macaroon on each of 6 dessert plates. Cover each macaroon with some diced pineapple and some Chantilly Cream. Repeat layering with another macaroon, pineapple, and cream. Top with the remaining macaroon. Serve immediately.

PLANNING AHEAD: The macaroons can be made a day ahead and stored at room temperature in an airtight container. The pineapple should be cut within a few hours of being eaten.

CUTTING PINEAPPLE

Choose a pineapple that isn't green and has a nice fragrance. (Once picked, a pineapple will not continue to ripen.) To core and cut a pineapple, slice off the top and bottom and place the pineapple on one end. Using a large chef's knife, start at the top of the pineapple and cut down along the sides between the flesh and the outer skin, removing the rind. Scoop out any remaining brown pieces with a paring knife. Again from the top, cut the pineapple into quarters. Place each piece on its side, core-side up. Horizontally cut off the core. Slice the pineapple flesh into pieces

frozen maple cream–pecan pie

Makes **6** servings

When I reflect on the person who gave me a recipe, making it takes on a deeper pleasure. Many recipes are not just printed words but also a personal connection. When I make Barbara Tropp's ginger ice cream with chocolate sauce, for example, it is as though she is by my side, peering over the top of her eyeglasses inspecting my work. When I make this adaptation of my grandmother's maple mousse recipe, I am transported back to Christmas on Crestwood Avenue in Corning, New York. I can feel the starch in the stiff white linen napkin resting in my lap as I sit at a long table full of cousins, aunts, and uncles. Through baking I can keep memories alive.

PECAN CRUST

   8 ounces (2 cups) pecans, toasted (see page 26)

   1 tablespoon brown sugar

   2 tablespoons granulated sugar

   1 $^1/_2$ ounces (3 tablespoons) unsalted butter, melted

MAPLE CREAM FILLING

   $^3/_4$ cup pure maple syrup

   1 large fresh egg white or pasteurized egg white (see Resources, page 182)

   Pinch of cream of tartar

   Pinch of salt

   1 cup heavy (whipping) cream

   Orange Cream Sauce (page 175)

Preheat the oven to 350 degrees F.

TO MAKE THE CRUST: Grind the pecans with the brown sugar and granulated sugar in a food processor. Transfer to a medium bowl and stir in the melted butter. Press the pecan mixture into the bottom and sides of a 9-inch pie pan. Bake 10 minutes.

TO MAKE THE FILLING: In a small saucepan over medium heat, bring the maple syrup to a boil and reduce to $^1/_2$ cup, about 5 minutes.

While the syrup is reducing, whip the egg white with an electric mixer on high speed until frothy. Add the cream of tartar and salt and whip until soft peaks form, 1 minute with a stand mixer or 3 minutes with a handheld mixer. (If the syrup reduces before the egg white has finished whipping, keep it warm over low heat.)

Pour the syrup into a glass measuring cup. With the mixer running, pour the maple syrup into the egg white in a thin steady stream. Mix for 30 seconds, turn off the motor, and scrape down the sides of the bowl. Whip on medium-high speed until thick and room temperature, about 3 minutes with a stand mixer or 5 minutes with a handheld mixer.

In a medium bowl, whip the cream until soft peaks form. Fold the cream into the cooled maple mixture. Spread it into the prepared piecrust. Freeze the pie for at least 4 hours to overnight.

TO SERVE: Cut into slices and serve with the Orange Cream Sauce.

PLANNING AHEAD: The pie can be made a day in advance and kept frozen.

double chocolate hot chocolate

Makes **6** 1-cup servings

This recipe is really dessert in a cup or truffle in a glass. It is very rich—just enough to fill a small espresso or demitasse cup is perfect. The different types of chocolate give it a deep flavor; adding a small amount of bitter cocoa powder cuts the sweetness. It is not for lightweights who prefer a mild-flavored hot chocolate. Serve a light tart for dessert and end the evening with this nonalcoholic nightcap.

1 $^1/_3$ cups heavy (whipping) cream
1 $^1/_2$ cups milk
11 ounces white chocolate, finely chopped
5 ounces milk chocolate, finely chopped
Pinch of salt
3 tablespoons cocoa powder

In a medium saucepan, warm the cream and milk over medium heat, stirring frequently, until hot and bubbling around the edges. Remove the pan from the heat and add the two chocolates, the salt, and the cocoa powder. Let sit for 15 seconds, then whisk until smooth.

Pour into espresso or demitasse cups and serve immediately.

PLANNING AHEAD: This hot chocolate can be made several days in advance. Refrigerate until ready to serve, then reheat in a microwave or double boiler.

hazelnut sandwich cookies

Makes about **32** cookies

Baking and decorating cookies signals the beginning of the winter holidays. Once the cookie cutters, sprinkles, and royal icing are on the counter, the season is officially launched. | Now that my nieces, nephews, and friends' kids are no longer babies, one of my new holiday traditions is a cookie party for adults and children. I notify guests in advance of the types of cookies I'm making and encourage them to bring cookies made from a favorite family recipe of their own. When people arrive, I have stacks of gingerbread people and other seasonal shapes baked and ready to frost. The aroma of cinnamon and ginger from the oven puts everyone in a holiday mood as the decorating begins. While the trays of decorated cookies grow and are admired, we all swap cookies and recipes. An added bonus of this get-together is that although each person may have only baked one kind of cookie, everyone gets to take several kinds home. | Here's a cookie to add to your favorite holiday recipes.

2 ounces ($^1/_2$ cup) hazelnuts, toasted and skins removed (see page 26)

1 $^1/_2$ cups all-purpose flour

5 ounces (10 tablespoons) unsalted butter, softened

2 ounces cream cheese

$^2/_3$ cup sugar

1 large egg

Pinch of salt

1 teaspoon baking powder

$^3/_4$ cup Nutella or your favorite jam, or as needed

In a food processor, finely grind the hazelnuts with $^1/_2$ cup of the flour.

Using an electric mixer on medium speed, beat together the butter, cream cheese, and sugar until light in color and smooth, 1 minute with a stand mixer or 2 minutes with a handheld mixer. Add the egg and mix until combined.

On low speed, add the ground hazelnuts, the remaining flour, the salt, and the baking powder and mix until smooth. Wrap the dough in plastic wrap and refrigerate for at least 1 hour.

Divide the dough into 4 pieces. On a lightly sugared work surface, roll the dough into 4 logs, each 8 inches long. Refrigerate for at least 1 hour until firm.

Preheat the oven to 350 degrees F. Line 2 baking sheets with parchment paper.

Slice the dough into $^1/_2$-inch-thick rounds. Place on the prepared baking sheets about 2 inches apart and bake until golden brown around the edges, about 8 minutes. Let cool to room temperature.

Sandwich 2 cookies together using about 1 teaspoon of Nutella or jam for each.

PLANNING AHEAD: The cookie dough can be made several days in advance and kept refrigerated. It can also be frozen. The cookies can be made several days in advance (without the filling). Store at room temperature in an airtight container. Sandwich the cookies the day you plan to serve them.

2 large eggs

3/4 cup sugar

3/4 cup buttermilk

1 tablespoon freshly squeezed Meyer lemon juice

Grated peel from 1 Meyer lemon

1 tablespoon heavy (whipping) cream

2 ounces (4 tablespoons) unsalted butter, melted

3 tablespoons flour

Pinch of salt

One 9-inch prebaked tart crust (page 170)

meyer lemon buttermilk tart

Makes **8** servings

California chefs are so mad for Meyer lemons that the bulk of the crop never makes it across the state line. A hybrid of the regular lemon, Meyers are sweeter, more aromatic, and less acidic. They have a softer yellow color and sometimes even a slight hint of orange in both the skin and flesh. They are a relatively new variety, imported from China to the United States by F. N. Meyer in 1908. Meyers are so ideal for desserts that I eagerly await the winter-spring season and mourn its passing once it's ended. To make sure that I never run out, I planted nine Meyer lemon trees along the front of my house. | Fortunately, commercial production is slowly increasing, so people in other parts of the country can begin to partake of this delectable lemon. If you can't find Meyer lemons, regular ones will work in this recipe. It wouldn't be a bad idea, however, to find a California pen pal to be your local source until you have an ample supply in your area.

Preheat the oven to 325 degrees F.

In a medium bowl, whisk together the eggs and sugar. Whisk in the buttermilk, lemon juice, lemon peel, cream, and melted butter. Whisk in the flour and salt.

Carefully pour the custard into the prebaked tart crust. Bake until the tart is set, about 35 minutes. Let cool to room temperature before cutting.

PLANNING AHEAD: Like all tarts, this is best made and eaten the same day.

triple chocolate trifles

Makes **6** servings

Practically speaking, trifles are very efficient desserts. They can (and actually should) be made ahead. They are self-contained to the point that the dessert, sauce, and garnish are all together in one bowl. This makes trifles great to prepare when you are taking dessert somewhere or are feeding a large crowd. More importantly, trifles are deliciously complex in flavor. All the components are wonderful on their own, but put them together and a heavenly flavor combination results. | Since chocolate is delectable in a dessert, I figured that a dessert that uses three kinds of chocolate would be three times as delicious. These individual trifles made with bittersweet, milk, and white chocolates will satisfy the most passionate chocoholics you know.

WHITE CHOCOLATE CREAM

1 3/4 cups heavy (whipping) cream

1/4 cup milk

1 vanilla bean, split lengthwise and seeds removed

6 ounces white chocolate, finely chopped

8 large egg yolks

2 tablespoons sugar

MILK CHOCOLATE CREAM

2 ounces milk chocolate, finely chopped

2 tablespoons water

1/2 cup heavy (whipping) cream

Indispensable Chocolate Cake, baked in an 8-inch square pan (page 176)

TO MAKE THE WHITE CHOCOLATE CREAM: Warm 3/4 cup of the cream, the milk, and the vanilla seeds and bean in a medium saucepan over medium heat until bubbles appear around the edges, about 5 minutes. Remove the pan from the heat and whisk in the white chocolate. Remove the vanilla bean.

In a large bowl, whisk together the egg yolks and sugar. Whisk in the white chocolate cream. Return the cream to the pan and cook over medium-low heat, stirring, until thick, 3 to 5 minutes. Be careful—as the cream cooks, it will thicken unevenly, getting thicker on the bottom first. Alternately stir the cream with a flat wooden spatula and a whisk to keep the mixture smooth. Cool over an ice bath (see page 28), stirring occasionally.

Whisk the remaining 1 cup cream until soft peaks form. Fold the whipped cream into the cooled white chocolate cream. Refrigerate for 30 minutes.

TO MAKE THE MILK CHOCOLATE CREAM: Melt the milk chocolate together with the water in a double boiler (see page 23). Whisk until smooth. Let cool to room temperature. If refrigerating it, stir occasionally, so that it cools smoothly.

Place the melted milk chocolate and the 1/2 cup cream in a bowl and whisk until soft peaks form. Refrigerate until you are ready to serve the trifle.

TO ASSEMBLE THE TRIFLE: Unmold the cake by running a knife around the inside edge of the pan and inverting it onto a work surface. Remove the pan and peel off the parchment paper. Using a drinking glass or a round cutter, cut the cake into 2 1/4 inch circles. Cut each circle in half. You will have 14 circles but will need only 12. In 6 tall glasses, alternately layer the White Chocolate Cream and the chocolate cake, ending with a layer of White Chocolate Cream. Cover each glass with plastic wrap and refrigerate for at least 1 hour. Just before serving, top with the Milk Chocolate Cream.

PLANNING AHEAD: The cake can be made a day in advance of assembling the trifle. The White Chocolate Cream can be made a day in advance and kept refrigerated. The Milk Chocolate Cream can be made several hours in advance.

1 $1/4$ cups all-purpose flour

$1/2$ teaspoon baking soda

$1/2$ teaspoon baking powder

$1/4$ teaspoon salt

2 teaspoons instant espresso powder

4 ounces (8 tablespoons) unsalted butter, softened

1 cup granulated sugar

2 large eggs

$1/2$ cup milk

MILK CHOCOLATE GANACHE

$2/3$ cup heavy (whipping) cream

5 $1/2$ ounces milk chocolate, finely chopped

WHITE CHOCOLATE FROSTING

4 $1/2$ ounces white chocolate, finely chopped

1 $3/4$ cups confectioners' sugar

$1/4$ cup milk

$1/2$ teaspoon vanilla extract

3 ounces (6 tablespoons) unsalted butter, softened

Pinch of salt

espresso cupcakes

WITH MILK CHOCOLATE GANACHE AND
WHITE CHOCOLATE FROSTING

Makes **12** cupcakes

I am frequently asked how I can be a pastry chef and not have to widen my front door to fit through it. I explain that desserts are like finances: I know when I can splurge and spend and when I must be frugal. I may save up for a pair of expensive designer shoes or buy a couple of pairs at once that are on sale. As I have a budget for shoes, I have a budget for desserts. I know how much and how often I can eat desserts and still fit into my favorite jeans. If I am having friends over for dinner, in the days preceding the party and the day after, I will forgo desserts and eat lightly. The day of the party, I will enjoy myself and not feel guilty or pay the price later on. If I overindulge over a period of time, I cut back on desserts until I am back on track. Some people feel that desserts are an all-or-nothing enterprise. They either eat them every day or never eat them. I say, we know we cannot afford every pair of shoes at the department store, but that doesn't mean we go barefoot! | I make these cupcakes (with two kinds of chocolate plus coffee) when I am in the mood for something decadent. They are worth the wait.

Preheat the oven to 350 degrees F. Line 12 cupcake wells with paper liners.

TO MAKE THE CUPCAKES: Sift together the flour, baking soda, baking powder, and salt. Stir in the espresso powder.

Using an electric mixer on medium speed, beat the butter with the granulated sugar until light, 1 minute with a stand mixer or 2 minutes with a handheld mixer. Add the eggs, one at a time, beating well after each addition. Continue to beat the mixture for 1 minute with a stand mixer or 2 minutes with a handheld mixer.

On low speed, alternately add the dry ingredients and the milk in 2 additions, stirring until incorporated after each addition.

Pour the batter into the paper-lined cupcake wells. Bake until a skewer inserted in the middle comes out clean, about 20 minutes. Let cool to room temperature, then remove from the pans.

TO MAKE THE GANACHE: Place the cream in a small, heavy-bottomed saucepan and warm over medium-high heat until it begins to bubble around the edges, about 5 minutes. Remove the pan from the stove, add the chocolate, and whisk until smooth. Transfer to a bowl and place plastic wrap directly over the ganache. Refrigerate until cold.

CONTINUED

TO MAKE THE FROSTING: Melt the white chocolate in a double boiler (see page 23). Stir until smooth. Let cool to room temperature.

Sift the confectioners' sugar into a medium bowl. Stir in the milk and vanilla. Add the butter and salt and beat until smooth. Stir in the cooled white chocolate. Refrigerate until firm enough to frost the cupcakes, about 30 minutes.

Cut out about one quarter of the inside of each cupcake with a small paring knife. Fill the indent with the milk chocolate ganache. Frost each cupcake with the white chocolate frosting.

PLANNING AHEAD: The cupcakes can be made a day in advance; wrap in plastic wrap and store at room temperature. The ganache can be made several days ahead and kept refrigerated. The frosting can be made a day ahead and stored at room temperature. For maximum flavor and moistness, fill and frost the cupcakes the day you plan to serve them.

rum caramel–
marinated oranges

OVER VANILLA BEAN ICE CREAM

Makes **8** servings

In the late 1600s in England, "orange girls" would sell oranges to theater patrons during intermission. In the 1800s, Laura Ingalls Wilder wrote about the thrill of receiving oranges in her Christmas stocking. During the long, hard Midwestern winter, she rarely saw any fresh fruit, let alone one that only grew thousands of miles away. Today it may seem hard to imagine her excitement, as oranges are abundant across the country year-round. Here is a simple recipe that takes the everyday orange and transforms it into an extraordinary dessert. After eating this, you, like Laura, won't take an orange for granted anymore.

6 large oranges
1 cup sugar
1/4 cup water
2 tablespoons dark rum
Vanilla Bean Ice Cream (page 179)

Peel and section the oranges into a medium bowl, to catch any juices. In a small bowl, squeeze any remaining juice out of the membrane. Reserve 6 tablespoons of the juice.

Cook the sugar and water in a medium saucepan over medium heat until the sugar dissolves, about 3 minutes. Increase to medium-high heat and continue to cook until the sugar is a light caramel color, about 5 minutes. Do not stir once the sugar begins to boil.

Remove the pan from the stove and add 1 tablespoon of the reserved orange juice. Gently stir the orange juice into the caramel, being careful, as the caramel will sputter. Stir in the rest of the orange juice, a tablespoon at a time. If at any time the caramel sputters violently, stop stirring until it subsides. Stir in the rum.

Pour the rum caramel over the orange sections. Marinate for at least 10 minutes to several hours.

TO SERVE: Scoop the Vanilla Bean Ice Cream into 8 bowls and top with the marinated oranges.

PLANNING AHEAD: The oranges can be sectioned a day in advance and kept refrigerated in their juices. The rum caramel can be made 2 days in advance and kept refrigerated. Reheat before adding the orange sections.

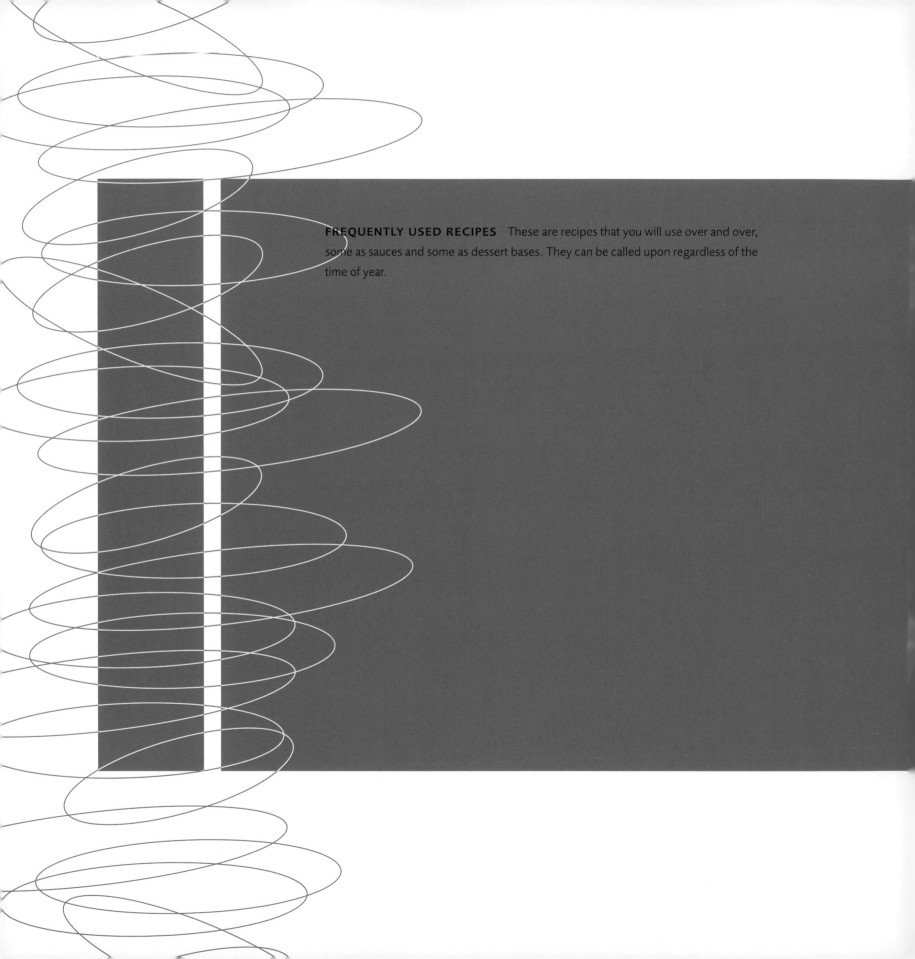

FREQUENTLY USED RECIPES These are recipes that you will use over and over, some as sauces and some as dessert bases. They can be called upon regardless of the time of year.

168   blitz puff pastry

169   crêpes

170   tart and pie doughs

172   chantilly cream

172   crème fraîche

173   caramel sauce

173   chocolate sauce

174   cinnamon cream

174   raspberry sauce

175   orange cream sauce

175   vanilla crème anglaise

176   indispensable chocolate cake

178   trifle cake

179   vanilla bean ice cream

180   ginger, cardamom, and cinnamon ice creams

180   candied nuts

2 cups all-purpose flour

$^1/_2$ teaspoon salt

12 ounces (24 tablespoons) cold European-style unsalted butter
(see page 22)

$^1/_2$ cup ice-cold water, or as needed

blitz puff pastry

Makes enough for **8** napoleons or **I** large tart

Professional cooking schools call rough puff pastry "blitz puff pastry." In this method, all the butter is cut into the flour instead of making a butter packet that is then wrapped and rolled inside a dough. European-style butter, with its higher fat content, is preferred in puff pastry. Fortunately, it is becoming easier to find in U.S. grocery stores (see Resources, page 182). Now home cooks can make blitz puff pastry equal to that made in fine restaurants and bakeries. | Once the initial dough is made, the recipe calls for rolling and folding (or "turning") the dough and letting it rest for an hour between turns. I wait to clean the flour off the counter until I am completely finished.

Stir together the flour and salt in a large bowl. Cut the butter into 1-inch pieces and add to the bowl. Using 2 knives or a pastry scraper, cut the butter into $^1/_4$-inch pieces as you mix it with the flour. Push the flour and butter out toward the edge of the bowl, making a hole in the center. Pour the ice-cold water into the hole. With your fingers, toss the flour, butter, and water together as though you were tossing a salad, until the water is evenly incorporated. The dough will not completely come together at this point.

Lay a large piece of plastic wrap on a work surface. Place the dough on the plastic wrap. If the dough still has bits of loose flour, sprinkle a little more ice-cold water and mix together with your fingers. At this point, the dough will be very loose but not dry. Place another piece of plastic wrap on top and gently press the dough together into an 8-by-6-inch rectangle. Wrap the plastic wrap around the dough and refrigerate until the butter is cold, at least 1 hour or up to 2 hours.

Lightly flour the work surface. Place the dough on the work surface and remove the plastic wrap. Press any loose pieces into the dough. Roll the dough into a 15-by-7-inch rectangle. Using a metal spatula or pastry scraper, make sure it is not sticking to the work surface. With a short end of the dough closest to you, fold it as you would a business letter: fold the top two-thirds of the dough toward you to the middle of the dough and then fold the bottom third over the top. Turn the dough on the work surface so the open fold is on your right and the closed seam on your left. Again roll the dough into a 15-by-7-inch rectangle and fold it like a business letter as before. It is not until this point that the dough will come together in one piece. Wrap the dough in plastic wrap and refrigerate until the butter is cold, at least 1 hour or up to 2 hours.

Repeat this process 2 more times, each time rolling and folding the dough twice and refrigerating it for an hour in between. Refrigerate the finished dough for 2 hours to several days before rolling into the shapes specified in each recipe.

PLANNING AHEAD: The puff pastry can be made a couple days in advance and kept refrigerated. It can also be frozen. Defrost in the refrigerator overnight before using.

crêpes

Makes **16** crêpes

Crêpes, thin French pancakes, are underutilized in this country as a basic dessert component. Ice cream, fruit throughout the year, toasted nuts, creamy fillings, and sauces can all be put on or in crêpes to create a multitude of distinctive desserts. Let your imagination be your guide. Replacing some of the flour with cornstarch produces lighter crêpes.

2 large eggs
$^1/_4$ cup water
I cup milk
$^3/_4$ cup all-purpose flour
6 tablespoons cornstarch
$^1/_4$ teaspoon cinnamon
$^1/_4$ teaspoon salt
I ounce (2 tablespoons) unsalted butter, melted
$^1/_2$ teaspoon vanilla extract

Whisk the eggs, water, and milk in a large bowl until combined. Sift together and then whisk in the flour, cornstarch, cinnamon, and salt. Whisk in the melted butter and vanilla. Refrigerate the batter for 30 minutes.

Heat a 6-inch crêpe pan or nonstick skillet over medium heat. Lightly grease the bottom of the pan. Fill a $^1/_4$ cup measure three-quarters full with the crêpe batter and pour it into the pan, rotating the pan so that a thin layer covers the entire bottom. Cook for about 1 $^1/_2$ minutes until lightly browned. Using the edge of a knife, loosen a corner of the crêpe from the pan. With your fingers, flip the crêpe over and cook for another 15 seconds. Place the finished crêpe on a large plate.

Continue cooking crêpes, stacking them, slightly overlapping, on top of each other, until there are at least 12 crêpes. It is not necessary to grease the pan after making each crêpe.

Wrap the crêpes in plastic wrap until ready to use. Store at room temperature for several hours but refrigerate overnight.

PLANNING AHEAD: Crêpes can be made ahead and kept refrigerated for up to 2 days or frozen for several weeks. Defrost for 30 minutes before using.

tart and pie doughs

Makes **I** 9-inch tart or **8** 4-inch tartlets.
Makes **I** 9-inch piecrust with lattice

Unlike most pastry chefs, I use all butter in both my tart and pie doughs. Many chefs use vegetable shortening or combine it with butter. The argument is that shortening adds flakiness. But if properly handled, an all-butter crust can be flaky and it has the added bonus of an all-butter flavor. When making dough, resist the urge to knead it too much. It should be handled just enough to form it into a smooth dough. Overworking will result in a tough crust. Too much liquid can also make dough tough. | In summer when it is very hot, I often use frozen butter to make my tart and pie dough. Cut cold butter into small pieces and freeze for 30 minutes to 1 hour before proceeding with the recipe. | Liquid is added to a dough to bring it together. In the two recipes following, I use water in one recipe and cream and egg in the other. Using water results in a more tender and more neutral-tasting dough. Cream and egg add some richness and flavor. Use whichever you prefer. The sole difference between a pie and a tart is the kind of pan used. A pie is made in a deeper pan with sloped sides and a tart in a shallower pan with fluted or straight sides.

TART DOUGH

I $1/2$ cups all-purpose flour

2 tablespoons sugar

Pinch of salt

5 ounces (10 tablespoons) cold unsalted butter

2 tablespoons heavy (whipping) cream

I large egg

TO MAKE THE DOUGH BY HAND: Combine the flour, sugar, salt, and butter in a large bowl. Using 2 knives or a pastry blender, mix in the butter until it is pea sized. In a small bowl, whisk together the cream and egg. Pour the cream mixture into the flour mixture and stir until the dough comes together.

TO MAKE THE DOUGH IN A FOOD PROCESSOR: Put the flour, sugar, salt, and butter in a food processor. In a small bowl, whisk together the cream and the egg. Pulse the flour mixture until the butter is pea sized. This will happen very quickly—be careful not to overprocess. With the machine running, pour the cream mixture into the food processor. Process just until the dough comes together.

TO MAKE THE DOUGH USING A STAND MIXER: Put the flour, sugar, salt, and butter in the bowl of an electric mixer. In a small bowl, whisk together the cream and egg. On low speed using the paddle attachment, mix in the butter until it is pea sized. Pour the cream mixture into the flour mixture and mix until the dough comes together.

Remove the dough from the bowl and form it into a 5 $1/2$-inch disk. Wrap in plastic wrap. Refrigerate for at least 30 minutes.

Place the dough on a lightly floured work surface. For a 9-inch tart, roll it out $1/8$ inch thick and cut it into a 12-inch circle. Drape the dough over the rolling pin and gently place it over the tart pan. Line the tart pan with the dough.

For individual tarts, roll the dough out $1/16$ inch thick and cut it into 6-inch circles. Reroll scraps to make 2 more. Line the tart pans with the dough.

Cut off any extra dough so it is flush with the top sides of the tart shells. Refrigerate for at least 30 minutes.

PREBAKING THE TART CRUST: Preheat the oven to 400 degrees F. Cut a parchment paper circle (or circles) large enough that it comes up several inches above the shell.

Line the tart shell(s) with the parchment paper circle(s). Fill with dried rice or dried beans. Bake until the edges of the crust are golden brown, about 20 minutes. Remove the parchment paper and rice and continue to bake for about 10 minutes until the bottom of the crust is golden brown.

(See facing page for planning ahead tips.)

PIE DOUGH

2 3/4 cups all-purpose flour

2 tablespoons sugar

Pinch of salt

8 ounces (16 tablespoons) cold unsalted butter

1/2 vanilla bean

5 to 6 tablespoons ice-cold water

TO MAKE THE DOUGH BY HAND: Combine the flour, sugar, salt, and butter. Cut the vanilla bean in half lengthwise. Scrape out the seeds and add them to the flour mixture; reserve the bean for another use. Using 2 knives or a pastry blender, mix together until the butter is pea sized. Pour the ice-cold water into the flour and mix just until the dough comes together.

TO MAKE THE DOUGH IN A FOOD PROCESSOR: Combine the flour, sugar, salt, butter, and vanilla seeds in the food processor bowl. Pulse the mixture until the butter is pea sized. This will happen very quickly—be careful not to overmix. With the machine running, pour the ice-cold water into the food processor. Process just until the dough begins to come together.

TO MAKE THE DOUGH USING A STAND MIXER: Put the flour, sugar, salt, butter, and vanilla seeds in the bowl of an electric mixer. On low speed using the paddle attachment, cut in the butter until it is pea sized. Pour in the ice-cold water and mix until the dough comes together.

Remove the dough from the bowl and press it together into a 5 1/2-inch disk. Wrap in plastic wrap and refrigerate for at least 30 minutes.

On a lightly floured work surface, roll two-thirds of the dough into an 11-inch circle, 3/16 inch thick. Line a 9-inch pie pan with the dough. Trim away excess dough. Roll the remaining dough 3/16 inch thick. Cut into 3/4-inch strips and save for the lattice top. Refrigerate the pie shell for at least 30 minutes.

PREBAKING THE PIECRUST: Preheat the oven to 400 degrees F. Cut a parchment paper circle 12 inches in diameter.

To prebake the piecrust, place the parchment paper circle on top of the dough in the pie pan and fill it with dried rice or beans. Bake until the edges of the crust are golden brown, about 20 minutes. Remove the parchment paper and weights and continue to bake until the bottom is golden brown, about 5 minutes.

PLANNING AHEAD: Tart and pie dough can be made several days in advance. If the dough has been in the refrigerator overnight, let it sit at room temperature for about 15 minutes, making it easier to roll out. Dough can be formed in the pan and kept refrigerated for up to 3 days and frozen for 3 weeks. For maximum flavor and flakiness, tarts and pies should be baked the day you are going to eat them.

Large, flat-bottomed coffee filters also work well as liners for prebaking tart and pie shells. Place the filter on top of the dough, making sure it is against the sides. Fill with dried beans or dried rice instead of pie weights, and then bake. Pie weights are more expensive.

chantilly cream

Makes **2** cups

Chantilly (pronounced "shahn-tee-yee" in France; "shan-ti-ly" in America) is French for "sweetened whipped cream." It has become a part of the American dessert menu vocabulary, as it is more poetic sounding. Some chefs use confectioners' sugar in their whipped cream, but I prefer granulated sugar, superfine if possible. Granulated sugar offers a cleaner taste. Do not add too much sugar or it will make the dessert you are serving it with taste too sweet. For flavoring you can add vanilla extract, vanilla seeds, or vanilla powder. | The appearance of Chantilly Cream should be smooth and satiny. If it is grainy looking, it has been overwhipped. Overwhipped cream, even by just a little bit, tastes dry and doesn't feel as creamy in the mouth. If you do overwhip cream, all is not lost: fold in a couple tablespoons of unwhipped cream and it will bring it back to the proper consistency. This won't work, however, if you have overwhipped it to the point where it has completely separated and looks like butter. If you don't have a whisk, you can whip cream by putting it in a jar and shaking it. Don't fill the jar more than half full, as heavy cream doubles in volume when whipped.

I cup heavy (whipping) cream
2 tablespoons sugar
$^1/_2$ teaspoon vanilla extract, seeds from $^1/_2$ vanilla bean,
 or $^1/_2$ teaspoon vanilla powder

Whisk the cream, sugar, and vanilla in a large bowl until soft peaks form. The cream should hold its shape but still be satiny in appearance. It should never be grainy (see headnote).

PLANNING AHEAD: Chantilly Cream can be refrigerated for several hours. It will lose a little of its thickness as it sits. The water separates and sinks to the bottom. The amount this happens depends on the variety of cream you are using. Before serving, lightly whisk it to bring it back to its original consistency. Always keep Chantilly Cream covered with plastic wrap. Cream absorbs other flavors easily.

crème fraîche

Makes about **2** cups

Crème fraîche is more widely available in U.S. grocery stores than it was a couple of years ago, but some stores still do not carry it. Luckily, it is simple enough to make—you just need to plan ahead to give it time to thicken. Powdered buttermilk does not work as well as the liquid variety. Crème fraîche is a tangy alternative to Chantilly Cream.

2 cups heavy (whipping) cream
2 tablespoons buttermilk

In a plastic container, stir together the cream and the buttermilk. Cover with an airtight lid and store at room temperature for 24 hours. Stir and cover. Again, let sit for 24 hours. If the crème fraîche is thick, refrigerate it. If it is still thin, let sit for another 24 hours.

TO WHIP CRÈME FRAÎCHE: Using an electric mixer, whisk until stiff. You can add a little sugar before whipping if desired.

PLANNING AHEAD: Crème fraîche will keep about 2 weeks in the refrigerator.

caramel sauce

Makes $1\frac{3}{4}$ cups

You can never have too much caramel sauce. Caramel is one of the few flavors that goes with everything. It has the intensity to stand up to other strong dessert flavors such as chocolate and coffee. At the same time, when paired with more delicate fruit flavors such as berries, pineapple, or pears, it doesn't overpower them.

$1\frac{1}{2}$ cups sugar

$\frac{1}{2}$ cup water

1 cup heavy (whipping) cream

$1\frac{1}{2}$ ounces (3 tablespoons) unsalted butter

In a medium saucepan, stir together the sugar and the water and cook over medium heat until the sugar has dissolved, about 5 minutes. Brush the insides of the pan with a pastry brush dipped in water to eliminate any sugar sticking to the sides. Increase to high heat and cook, without stirring, until the sugar is amber colored, 8 to 10 minutes. Remove the pan from the heat.

Wearing oven mitts, slowly add $\frac{1}{4}$ cup of the cream. Be careful, as the caramel will sputter as the cream is added. Using a wooden spoon or heat-resistant spatula, stir the cream into the caramel. If the cream sputters, stop stirring. Let the bubbles subside and then stir again. Carefully add the remaining cream. Stir until combined. Cool 5 minutes and then whisk in the butter.

Let cool to room temperature and then refrigerate. Reheat in a double boiler or microwave.

PLANNING AHEAD: Caramel sauce can be made up to a week in advance and kept refrigerated.

chocolate sauce

Makes $1\frac{3}{4}$ cups

Chocolate sauce is always good to have on hand. It can liven up store-bought ice cream or be used as a sauce on caramel, chocolate, nut, or coffee desserts. Be sure to use bittersweet chocolate for the best flavor.

1 cup heavy (whipping) cream

10 ounces bittersweet chocolate, finely chopped

In a small saucepan, bring the cream to a low boil over medium heat, about 5 minutes. Turn off the heat, add the chocolate, and cover the pan. Let steep for 5 minutes.

Stir the sauce until smooth. Serve as specified in the recipe.

PLANNING AHEAD: The sauce can be made several days in advance and kept refrigerated.

cinnamon cream

Makes 2 1/2 cups

The best of Chantilly Cream with a little something extra.

1 1/4 cups heavy (whipping) cream
3 tablespoons sugar
1/8 teaspoon ground cinnamon

Combine all of the ingredients and whisk until soft peaks form. Refrigerate until you are ready to use.

PLANNING AHEAD: Cinnamon cream can be made several hours ahead. It will lose a little of its thickness as it sits. The water separates and sinks to the bottom. Before serving, lightly whisk it to bring it back to its original consistency. Cover with plastic wrap and refrigerate until ready to use.

raspberry sauce

Makes about 3/4 cup

A great, versatile sauce—you can substitute other berries, peaches, or plums.

12-ounce bag frozen raspberries (no sugar added), defrosted
2 tablespoons sugar, or as needed

Puree the raspberries in a food processor. Strain the puree through a fine-mesh sieve into a bowl, discarding the seeds. Stir in the sugar. Taste for sweetness and add another tablespoon of sugar if needed. Refrigerate until ready to use.

PLANNING AHEAD: Raspberry sauce will keep for several days in the refrigerator.

orange cream sauce

Makes $1\frac{1}{2}$ cups

A thick sauce with a slightly bitter orange flavor.

2 tablespoons sugar
2 large egg yolks
$\frac{1}{2}$ cup freshly squeezed orange juice
$1\frac{1}{4}$ cups heavy (whipping) cream
Grated peel from 1 orange

In a medium bowl, whisk together the sugar and egg yolks until combined.

Cook the orange juice in a medium saucepan over medium heat until the juice reduces to about 1 1/2 tablespoons, about 5 minutes. Stir in the cream. Cook until the cream begins to boil around the edges, about 3 minutes.

Slowly whisk the orange cream into the egg yolks. Pour the cream back into the pan and cook over low heat, stirring constantly with a heat-resistant rubber spatula or the end of a flat wooden spoon, until the sauce thickens and coats the back of a spoon, 3 to 5 minutes. Strain the sauce and stir in the orange peel. Cool over an ice bath (see page 28) until cold. Refrigerate until you are ready to serve.

PLANNING AHEAD: The sauce can be made a day in advance and kept refrigerated.

vanilla crème anglaise

Makes $1\frac{1}{2}$ cups

Like Chantilly Cream, crème anglaise is a common dessert sauce. They both have a neutral flavor that helps to highlight and contrast with the other components of a dessert. Often you can use either in a dessert but sometimes crème anglaise is the better choice. A perfect example of this is when it is used with the Walnut Cake with Chocolate Orange Sabayon (page 129). Without some crème anglaise, the dessert would taste too intense and it would be difficult to eat a whole portion. Because it has less fat than Chantilly Cream, Vanilla Crème Anglaise adds a flavor balance without adding more richness.

5 large egg yolks
2 tablespoons sugar
Pinch of salt
$1\frac{1}{2}$ cups milk
1 vanilla bean, split lengthwise and seeds removed

Whisk the egg yolks, sugar, and salt in a medium bowl until smooth.

Warm the milk, and the vanilla bean and seeds in a medium saucepan over medium heat, stirring occasionally, until hot and bubbling around the edges, about 5 minutes. Slowly whisk the milk into the egg mixture. Pour the milk back into the pan. Cook over low heat, stirring continuously, until it thickens slightly and coats a metal or wooden spoon with a thin film, about 10 minutes.

Strain the custard into a bowl, discarding the vanilla bean. Cool over an ice bath (see page 28). Refrigerate for at least 30 minutes.

PLANNING AHEAD: Vanilla Crème Anglaise can be made up to 2 days in advance and kept refrigerated.

indispensable chocolate cake

Makes **1** 8- or 9-inch cake

There are some recipes in my repertoire that I repeatedly use in different ways. The following chocolate cake recipe is a perfect example. I use it for the Chocolate Chip Ice Cream Cake (page 78), Triple Chocolate Trifles (page 161), The Coffee Chocolate Towers (page 44), and the Individual German Chocolate Cakes (page 108). I originally thought it was necessary to have a new cake recipe for each of these desserts, but then I got smart. If you are familiar with a recipe and it works consistently, you can reincarnate it in as many ways as possible. Properly designed, each dessert tastes unique and you won't even recognize that you are eating the same cake.

FOR CHOCOLATE CHIP ICE CREAM CAKE AND INDIVIDUAL GERMAN CHOCOLATE CAKE

1/2 cup cocoa powder

3/4 cup all-purpose flour

1/4 teaspoon baking powder

1/8 teaspoon salt

4 ounces (8 tablespoons) unsalted butter, softened

1 cup plus 2 tablespoons sugar

3 large eggs

6 tablespoons buttermilk

3/4 teaspoon vanilla extract

FOR COFFEE CHOCOLATE TOWERS AND TRIPLE CHOCOLATE TRIFLES

1/4 cup cocoa powder

6 tablespoons all-purpose flour

1/8 teaspoon baking powder

Pinch of salt

2 ounces (4 tablespoons) unsalted butter, softened

1/2 cup sugar

2 large eggs

3 tablespoons buttermilk

1/2 teaspoon vanilla extract

Preheat the oven to 350 degrees F.

FOR ALL CAKES: Spray an 8-inch square pan with cooking oil spray. Line the bottom with parchment paper.

TO MAKE THE CAKE: Sift together the cocoa powder, flour, baking powder, and salt.

With an electric mixer, cream together the butter and sugar until smooth, about 1 minute with a stand mixer or 2 minutes with a handheld mixer. Add the eggs one at a time, beating for 15 seconds after each addition.

In a small bowl or measuring cup, stir together the buttermilk and vanilla. On low speed, add one-third of the cocoa and flour mixture to the butter and sugar mixture, mixing until combined. Add half of the buttermilk and mix well. Repeat, alternating the dry and wet mixtures, combining each set of ingredients before adding the next. Evenly spread the batter into the prepared cake pan.

FOR CHOCOLATE CHIP ICE CREAM CAKE AND THE INDIVIDUAL GERMAN CHOCO-LATE CAKES: Bake in the prepared 8-inch pan until a skewer inserted in the middle comes out clean, about 25 minutes.

FOR TRIPLE CHOCOLATE TRIFLES AND COFFEE CHOCOLATE TOWERS: Bake in the prepared 8-inch square pan until a skewer inserted in the middle comes out clean, about 15 minutes.

Let the cake cool in the pan to room temperature.

PLANNING AHEAD: The chocolate cake can be made a day in advance; wrap in plastic wrap and store at room temperature.

1 1/4 cups all-purpose flour

2 1/2 teaspoons baking powder

Pinch of salt

5 large eggs, separated

1 1/4 cups sugar

5 tablespoons very hot water

1 1/2 teaspoons vanilla extract

trifle cake

Makes **1** 15-by-10-by-1-inch cake

Some people like to use ladyfingers in their trifles, but I find that they become too soggy and disintegrate when combined with creams and sauces. I prefer to use a cake with more of a spongy texture. This cake is also called sponge cake. As its name implies, it feels a little spongy and can soak up liquid but still retain its shape. In this recipe, you can add grated citrus zest, ground spices, or instant powdered coffee to complement any trifles you dream up.

Preheat the oven to 350 degrees F. Grease the bottom of a 15-by-10-by-1-inch jelly-roll pan and line the bottom with parchment paper.

Sift together the flour, baking powder, and salt.

In a medium bowl with an electric mixer, whip together the egg yolks and sugar on high speed until thick and smooth, about 2 minutes with a stand mixer or 4 minutes with a handheld mixer. Reduce to low speed and add the hot water and vanilla. Scrape down the sides of the bowl. Again increase to high speed and whip until thick, about 1 minute.

On low speed, stir in the dry ingredients.

In another bowl with an electric mixer, whip the egg whites until soft peaks form, 1 minute with a stand mixer or 2 to 3 minutes with a handheld mixer. Fold the egg whites into the batter. Spread the batter evenly and gently into the prepared pan.

Bake the cake until it is golden brown in color and springs back lightly when touched on top, about 20 minutes. Let it cool to room temperature. Remove the cake by running a knife around the inside edge of the pan and inverting it onto a counter. Lift the pan and carefully peel off the parchment paper.

PLANNING AHEAD: The cake can be made several days in advance; wrap in plastic wrap and store at room temperature. The cake is easier to cut if it is a day old.

vanilla bean ice cream

Makes 1 1/2 quarts

Without vanilla bean ice cream, many desserts would not reach their full potential. When used with fruit desserts, it adds creaminess and texture. With chocolate or nut desserts, it balances their richness. With warm desserts, cold ice cream is a heavenly pairing. There are many ways to make ice cream: with or without eggs, with all cream, or with part cream and part milk. All can be equally delicious depending on what it is ultimately being served with. For a delicious all-around vanilla bean ice cream that can be served by itself or with most desserts, I prefer this recipe. There are days, however, when I just don't have time to make it. Luckily, there are a few good vanilla bean ice creams available in stores.

ICE CREAM BASE

8 large egg yolks

3/4 cup sugar

1/4 teaspoon salt

2 cups milk

2 1/2 cups heavy (whipping) cream

1 vanilla bean, split lengthwise and seeds removed

Whisk together the egg yolks, 1/2 cup of the sugar, and the salt in a large stainless-steel bowl until combined.

In a medium saucepan, cook the remaining 1/4 cup sugar, the milk, the cream, and the vanilla bean and seeds over medium-high heat, stirring until it bubbles around the edges, about 5 minutes. Turn off the heat, cover, and let steep for 5 minutes.

Slowly whisk the cream mixture into the egg yolks. Pour the egg-cream mixture back into the pan. Cook over medium-low heat, stirring constantly with a heat-proof rubber spatula until it coats the back of the spatula, about 3 minutes. Pour the mixture into a clean bowl and cool over an ice bath (see page 28) to room temperature. Refrigerate until cold, 2 hours to overnight.

Strain through a medium-mesh sieve, discarding the vanilla bean, and freeze in an ice cream machine according to the manufacturer's instructions. Transfer the ice cream to a container and place plastic wrap directly on top of the ice cream. Freeze until ready to serve.

PLANNING AHEAD: The ice cream base can be made a day or two in advance and kept refrigerated. The ice cream can be frozen several days in advance.

If you have the type of ice cream machine with the separate Freon unit that must be frozen before making ice cream, buy an extra one. With two, you can make two batches of ice cream in a row and not have to wait for the unit to refreeze. Store at least one of them in the freezer.

ginger, cardamom, and cinnamon ice creams

A basic vanilla bean ice cream can be used as a base for many other flavors. Start out with the variations listed below. You can also infuse toasted nuts or citrus peel in the custard or add finely chopped chocolate to the hot custard. | Follow the Vanilla Bean Ice Cream recipe (page 179). For each flavor, add the following ingredients with the vanilla bean:

FOR GINGER ICE CREAM

3 ounces fresh gingerroot, cut into 1-inch pieces

FOR CARDAMOM ICE CREAM

1 teaspoon ground cardamom

FOR CINNAMON ICE CREAM

1 cinnamon stick
1/8 teaspoon cinnamon

candied nuts

Makes **2** cups

Candied nuts are a terrific generic garnish for many desserts. They add crunch to creamy desserts and height to flat ones. Depending on the flavor of the dessert, I use a wide variety of nuts—almonds, macadamia nuts, pecans, or walnuts. They all work well. For added flavor, feel free to add ground spices such as cinnamon, cardamom, or ginger to the egg white before whisking.

1 large egg white
3 tablespoons sugar
8 ounces (2 cups) nuts

Preheat the oven to 325 degrees F. In a medium bowl, whisk the egg white and sugar just until combined. With a rubber spatula, gently stir in the nuts. Spread the nut mixture in a single layer on an unlined baking sheet.

Bake, stirring every 5 minutes with a metal spatula, being sure to scrape any sugar pieces off the bottom of the tray, until the nuts are dry, 15 to 20 minutes. Let cool to room temperature. Store in an airtight container.

PLANNING AHEAD: Candied nuts will keep for 2 weeks in an airtight container.

resources

INFORMATION

You can find general information about ingredients on the following Web sites.

almonds
ALMOND BOARD OF CALIFORNIA: www.almondsarein.com

apples
WASHINGTON STATE APPLE COMMISSION: www.bestapples.com
CALIFORNIA APPLE COMMISSION: www.calapple.org

blueberries
NORTH AMERICAN BLUEBERRY COUNCIL: www.blueberry.org

butter
www.butterisbest.com

cherries
CHERRY MARKETING INSTITUTE: www.cherrymkt.org
CALIFORNIA CHERRY ADVISORY BOARD: www.calcherry.com
NORTHWEST CHERRY ASSOCIATION: www.nwcherries.com

dairy
DAIRY COUNCIL OF CALIFORNIA: www.dairycouncilofca.org

eggs
AMERICAN EGG BOARD: www.aeb.org

farmers' markets
www.ams.usda.gov/farmersmarkets

pears
CALIFORNIA PEAR ADVISORY BOARD: www.calpear.com

pistachios
CALIFORNIA PISTACHIO COMMISSION: www.pistachios.org

strawberries
CALIFORNIA STRAWBERRY COMMISSION: www.calstrawberry.com

vanilla
THE VANILLA COMPANY: www.vanilla.com

EQUIPMENT AND INGREDIENTS

You will find quality equipment and ingredients at these retail stores, catalogs, and Web sites.

Beryl's Cake Decorating Equipment

(703) 256-6951

www.beryls.com

Cake-decorating products.

Bridge Kitchenware

(800) 274-3435

(212) 838-6746

www.bridgekitchenware.com

Baking and cooking equipment.

Chef's Catalogue

(800) 338-3232

www.chefscatalog.com

Baking and cooking equipment.

Chocolates El Rey

(800) 357-3999

www.chocolate-elrey.com

Fine chocolate.

Chocosphere

www.chocosphere.com

Callebaut, El Rey, Green and Black, Michel Cluizel, Scharffen Berger, and Valrhona chocolates. Michel Cluizel, Green and Black, and Valrhona cocoa powders.

Cookie Cutters Etc.

(805) 484-4989

www.cookiecuttersetc.com

Cookie cutters.

Dean & Deluca

(800) 221-7714

www.dean-deluca.com

Baking (and other cooking) ingredients and equipment.

Doughmakers Bakeware

(888) 386-8517

www.doughmakers.com

Bakeware and baking information.

Eggology

(888) 669-6557

www.eggology.com

Pasteurized egg whites.

Ginger People

(Royal Pacific Foods)

(800) 551-5284

www.gingerpeople.com

Candied ginger.

Guittard Chocolate

www.guittard.com

Fine chocolate.

J. B. Prince

(800) 473-0577

www.jbprince.com

Professional cooking equipment.

Kerekes Equipment

(800) 525-5556

www.kerekesequip.com

Baking equipment.

King Arthur Flour

(800) 827-6836

www.kingarthurflour.com

Baking ingredients and equipment.

KitchenAid

www.kitchenaid.com

Products and baking information.

Kitchen Collectables

(888) 593-2436

www.kitchencollectables.com

Cookie cutters.

Lee's Market

www.leesmarket.com

Specialty foods.

New York Cake & Baking Distributor

(800) 942-2539

(212) 675-2253

Baking equipment.

Nielsen-Massey Vanillas

(800) 525-7873

www.nielsenmassey.com

Vanilla beans, extracts, pastes, and powders.

Pasteurized Egg Co.

(800) 410-7619

www.safeeggs.com

Pasteurized eggs, in the shell.

Penzey's Spices

(800) 741-7787

www.penzeys.com

High-quality spices.

Perfect Puree

(800) 556-3707

www.perfectpuree.com

Fruit purees and juice without any added sugar.

Pfeil and Holing

(802) 247-7955

www.cakedeco.com

Cake-decorating supplies.

Sur La Table

(800) 243-0852

www.surlatable.com

Cooking equipment and tableware.

Sweet Celebrations

(800) 328-6722

www.sweetc.com

Baking equipment and ingredients.

Williams-Sonoma

(800) 541-2233

www.williams-sonoma.com

Cooking equipment and tableware.

Zabars

(800) 697-6301

www.zabars.com

Cooking equipment and ingredients.

bibliography

To say I am a book enthusiast is putting it mildly. I adore books of all types but especially cookbooks. If I meander into a bookstore to pass some time before an appointment, I inevitably come out with several books under my arm. I am like a kid in a candy store—I desire everything and have a difficult time deciding. Once home, I am perfectly content to sit for days on end with my sole companion a pile of cookbooks.

I ask potential employees during interviews what three cookbooks they would take with them to a desert island and why. The answers are always interesting and always varied.

Here are the cookbooks I referenced in writing this cookbook and some I find myself going back to time after time.

Alexander, Stephanie. *Stephanie's Seasons*. St. Leonards, Australia: Rathdowne, 1993.

Ammer, Christine. *Fruitcakes and Couch Potatoes and Other Delicious Expressions*. New York: Penguin Books, 1992.

Baker's Dozen, The. *The Baker's Dozen Cookbook*. New York: William Morrow, 2001.

Barnette, Martha. *Ladyfingers and Nun's Tummies—A Lighthearted Look at How Foods Got Their Names*. New York: Times Books, 1997.

Bloom, Carole. *All About Chocolate*. New York: Macmillan, 1998.

———. *The International Dictionary of Desserts, Pastries, and Confections*. New York: William Morrow, 1995.

Coe, Sophie D., and Michael D. Coe *The True History of Chocolate*. New York: Thames and Hudson, 1996.

Corriher, Shirley. *Cookwise*. New York: William Morrow, 1997.

Daley, Regan. *In the Sweet Kitchen—The Definitive Baker's Guide*. New York: Artisan, 2001.

Damerow, Gail. *Ice Cream! The Whole Scoop*. Macomb, IL: Glenbridge Press, 1991.

David, Elizabeth. *Harvest of the Cold Months*. New York: Penguin Books, 1994.

Davidson, Alan. *The Oxford Companion to Food*. Oxford England: Oxford University Press, 1999.

De'Medici, Lorenza. *A Passion for Fruits*. New York: Abbeville Press, 2000.

Escoffier, Auguste. *Le Guide Culinaire*. New York: Mayflower Books, 1921.

Friberg, Bo. *The Professional Pastry Chef*, 2nd ed. New York: Van Nostrand Reinhold, 1990.

Gage, Fran. *Bread and Chocolate*. Seattle: Sasquatch Books, 1999.

Gibbs, Barbara Ostmann. *The Recipe Writer's Handbook*. New York: John Wiley and Sons, 2001.

Herbst, Sharon Tyler. *Food Lover's Companion*. New York: Barrons Educational Series, 1990.

———. *Never Eat More Than You Can Lift*. New York: Broadway Books, 1997.

Kimball, Chris. *The Dessert Bible*. New York: Little, Brown and Company, 2000.

Lamott, Anne. *Bird by Bird*. New York: Anchor Books, 1995.

Mariani, John. *Encyclopedia of American Food and Drink*. New York: Lebhar-Friedman, 1999.

Metropolitan Museum of Art. *Victorian Ices and Ice Creams*. New York: Charles Scribner's Sons, 1976

Mintz, Sidney W. *Sweetness and Power—The Place of Sugar in Modern History*. New York: Penguin Books, 1985.

Riely, Elizabeth. *A Feast of Fruits*. New York: Macmillan, 1993

Rombauer, Irma S., Marion Rombauer-Becker, and Ethan Becker. *The New Joy of Cooking*. New York: Scribner, 1997.

Sonnenfeld, Albert, Jean-Louis Flandrin, and Massimo Montanari. *Food, A Culinary History from Antiquity to the Present*. New York: Columbia University Press, 1999.

Stevens, Patricia Bunning. *Rare Bits*. Athens, OH: Ohio University Press, 1998.

Toussaint-Samat, Maguelonne. Translated by Anthea Bell. *A History of Food*. Cambridge, MA: Blackwell Publishers, 1992.

Trager, James. *The Food Chronology*. New York: Henry Holt and Company, 1997.

Visser, Margaret. *The Rituals of Dinner*. New York: Grove Weidenfeld, 1991.

Walheim, Lance. *Citrus*. Tuscon, AZ: Ironwood Press, 1996.

Wilson, C. Anne. *The Book of Marmalade*. New York: St. Martin's, 1985.

Wolf, Burt. *Gatherings and Celebrations*. New York: Doubleday, 1996.

Wolf, Burt, Emily Aronson, and Florence Fabricant. *The New Cook's Catalogue*. New York: Alfred A. Knopf, 2000.

acknowledgments

Thanks to my friends and family, who welcomed me with open arms (even though they really wanted to lock the door and pretend they weren't at home) when they saw me coming up their front walks, arms laden with more variations of desserts to try.

Special thanks to everyone at Farallon for creating an inspirational food and service team. Dena Deville and Jennifer Creager for keeping the pastry department running so smoothly. Mark Franz, Parke Ulrich, Nathan Powers, Heather Ames, Karen Bell, and Nicole Lago on the savory side, and the front of the house managers: Tyler Williams, Julie Ring, Sharon Yeager, Chris Durie, Michael Musil, and Peter Palmer. Pat Kuleto for creating such an incredible interior. The entire Farallon staff was tireless in its willingness to eat my experiments at family meals.

Each recipe in this book has been tested many times not just by me but also by home cooks. Thanks to Angela Brassinga, Paula McShane Conway, Laurinda DeFlorio, Janet Egan, Abby Greenup, Suzie Greenup, Nancy Luchetti, Mary Sue Murray, Kate Petcavich, Erin Loftus Sweetland, Renée Toomire, Ingrid Ulrich, Lisa Weiss, and Kristina Wun.

Thanks also to:
Minh + Wass and stylist Susie Theodorou, for the exquisite photographs that make the desserts look as enticing on the printed page as they do in real life.

Jane Dystel, for being my agent.

Don Horton, for helping the delivery people get my stove down the driveway to launch this book and for his readiness to take the overflow of desserts off my hands.

Adair Lara, for taking out all the unnecessary words and making what was left clearer.

Bill LeBlond, for his positive and enthusiastic support.

Andy Powning from Greenleaf Produce, for answering my frequent one-line e-mail queries with several paragraphs.

Sara Schneider for her gorgeous book design.

Janet Rikala, for her editing expertise.

Amy Treadwell for her attention to detail.

And finally, all the pastry chefs I have worked with at Stars and Farallon: Earl Darny, Tim Grable, Don Hall, Julia Orenstein, Elizabeth Scherber, Hollyce Snyder, Darcy Tizio, Jules Vranian, and Carolyn Weil.

index

A

Almonds, 35, 182
    Apricot Jalousie Tart, 66
    Baked Pears with Almond Streusel, 35
    Bing Cherry Filo Rolls with Cardamom Ice
        Cream, 72
    Cinnamon Panna Cotta, 50
    Milk Chocolate Cheesecake, 47
    Raspberry Ice Cream Sandwiches, 151–52
    toasting, 26
    Vanilla Almond Savarin with Ginger Ice Cream
        Balls, 53–54
Apples, 104, 182
    Apple Caramel Bread Pudding, 137
    Apple Compote, 104
    Apple Filo Napoleons, 63
    Apple–Olive Oil Cake, 98
    Apple Splits, 102
    Autumn "Summer" Pudding, 99
    Cinnamon Apple Crêpes, 104–5
    cutting, 29
    Fifty-Year Apple Cake, 36
    Grandmother's Apple Cake, 112
Apricot Jalousie Tart, 66
Autumn "Summer" Pudding, 99

B

Baked Pears with Almond Streusel, 35
Baking powder, 22
Baking soda, 22
Bananas, 138
    Banana Cream–Graham Cracker Napoleons, 134
    Hot Buttered Rum and Banana Compote with
        Vanilla Bean Ice Cream, 138
Bars, Walnut Hazelnut, 61–62
Berries, 69. *See also individual berries*
    Berry Crème Fraîche Cake, 69–70
    Berry Sauce, 86
    Best-of-Summer Shortcakes, 67
    Mascarpone Custard with Summer Fruits, 81
    Red Berry–White Chocolate Trifles, 86–88
Best-of-Summer Shortcakes, 67
Bing Cherry Filo Rolls with Cardamom Ice Cream,
    72

Bittersweet Chocolate Fondue, 135
Bittersweet Chocolate Mousse Cake with White
    Chocolate Sauce, 139
Blackberry-Peach Compote, 77
Black Forest Brownies with Mocha Ganache, 74
Black Mission Fig Honey Cake, 37
Blitz Puff Pastry, 168
Blueberries, 182
    Berry Crème Fraîche Cake, 69–70
    Blueberry Compote, 84
    Blueberry Sauce, 82
    Peach Blueberry Trifle, 84
    Rustic Blueberry Tart, 93
Bombe, Three-Melon Sorbet, 91–92
Bourbon Milk Shake, 40
Brandy Snaps, 141
Bread
    Apple Caramel Bread Pudding, 137
    Autumn "Summer" Pudding, 99
    Lemon-Raspberry Bread Pudding, 80
    Triple-Layer Pear Brioche Sandwiches, 111
Brownies, Black Forest, with Mocha Ganache, 74
Brown Sugar Meringues with Strawberries, 38
Butter, 22, 182

C

Cakes
    Apple–Olive Oil Cake, 98
    Berry Crème Fraîche Cake, 69–70
    Bittersweet Chocolate Mousse Cake with White
        Chocolate Sauce, 139
    Black Mission Fig Honey Cake, 37
    Chocolate Chip Ice Cream Cake, 78
    Citrus Cake, 146–47
    Coffee Chocolate Towers, 44
    cutting, 29
    Fifty-Year Apple Cake, 36
    Grandmother's Apple Cake, 112
    Indispensable Chocolate Cake, 176–77
    Individual German Chocolate Cakes, 108–9
    Orange Pound Cake with Concord Grape
        Compote, 114
    Poppy Seed Cake, 69
    Pumpkin Cake, 122–23

Pumpkin Upside-Down Cake with Cranberry
Pecan Topping, 120
Trifle Cake, 178
Walnut Cake with Chocolate Orange Sabayon
and Vanilla Crème Anglaise, 129–30
Candied Ginger Shortbread Stacks with Peach-
Blackberry Compote, 77
Candied Nuts, 180
Cantaloupe Sorbet, 91
Cappuccino Custard with Cinnamon Cream, 75
Caramel
Apple Caramel Bread Pudding, 137
Caramel Chocolate-Chunk Tart, 43
Caramel Panna Cotta, 50
Caramel Pecan Sauce, 108
Caramel Sauce, 173
making, 28
Pear–Caramel Swirl Ice Cream with Pecan
Cookies, 117–18
Rum Caramel–Marinated Oranges over Vanilla
Bean Ice Cream, 165
Cardamom Ice Cream, 180
Cassis Sauce, 41
Chantilly Cream, 172
Cheese
Mascarpone Custard with Summer Fruits, 81
Milk Chocolate Cheesecake, 47
Ricotta Cheesecake with Dried Cherries and
Golden Raisins, 127
Cherries, 182
Bing Cherry Filo Rolls with Cardamom Ice Cream,
72
Black Forest Brownies with Mocha Ganache, 74
pitting, 19, 72
Ricotta Cheesecake with Dried Cherries and
Golden Raisins, 127
Chestnut Chocolate Marquise, 149–50
Chocolate, 22–23, 139
Bittersweet Chocolate Fondue, 135
Bittersweet Chocolate Mousse Cake with White
Chocolate Sauce, 139
Black Forest Brownies with Mocha Ganache, 74
Caramel Chocolate-Chunk Tart, 43
Chestnut Chocolate Marquise, 149–50

Chocolate Chip Ice Cream Cake, 78
Chocolate Glaze, 44
Chocolate Mocha Truffles, 143
Chocolate Orange Sabayon, 129–30
Chocolate–Peanut Butter Milk Shake, 71
Chocolate–Peanut Butter Truffles, 144
Chocolate Sauce, 173
Coffee Chocolate Towers, 44
Double Chocolate Hot Chocolate, 157
Indispensable Chocolate Cake, 176–77
Individual German Chocolate Cakes, 108–9
melting, 23
Milk Chocolate Cheesecake, 47
Milk Chocolate Cream, 161
Milk Chocolate Ganache, 163
Mocha Ganache, 74
Pumpkin Zuccotto, 122–23
Triple Chocolate Trifles, 161
Cinnamon
Cinnamon Apple Crêpes, 104–5
Cinnamon Cream, 174
Cinnamon Ice Cream, 180
Cinnamon Marsala Sabayon, 125–26
Cinnamon Panna Cotta, 50
Citrus fruits, 146. See also individual fruits
Citrus Cake, 146–47
Citrus Compote, 141–42
Citrus Glaze, 146–47
Cocoa powder, 23
Coconut, 23–24
Coconut Meringues, 55
Coconut Pastry Cream, 108
Coconut Pavlovas with Lime Curd, Ginger Ice
Cream, and Papayas, 55
Individual German Chocolate Cakes, 108–9
Macaroon Pineapple Napoleons, 155
toasting, 24
Coffee, 24
Cappuccino Custard with Cinnamon Cream, 75
Chocolate Mocha Truffles, 143
Coffee Chocolate Towers, 44
Espresso Cupcakes with Milk Chocolate
Ganache and White Chocolate Frosting,
163–64

Mocha Ganache, 74
White Chocolate Coffee Mousse, 44
Compotes
Apple Compote, 104
Blueberry Compote, 84
Citrus Compote, 141–42
Concord Grape Compote, 114
Hot Buttered Rum and Banana Compote, 138
Peach-Blackberry Compote, 77
Strawberry Rhubarb Compote, 48
Concord Grape Compote, 114
Cookies
Brandy Snaps, 141
Figamaroles, 119
Hazelnut Sandwich Cookies, 158
Lime Cookies, 85
Pecan Cookies, 117–18
Walnut Hazelnut Bars, 61–62
Cooking oil spray, 24
Corn Crêpes with Blueberry Sauce and Vanilla
Bean Ice Cream, 82
Cranberry Pecan Topping, Pumpkin Upside-
Down Cake with, 120
Cream, 24
Chantilly Cream, 172
Cinnamon Cream, 174
Milk Chocolate Cream, 161
White Chocolate Cream, 161
Crème Anglaise, Vanilla, 175
Crème fraîche, 24, 172
Crêpes, 169
Cinnamon Apple Crêpes, 104–5
Corn Crêpes with Blueberry Sauce and Vanilla
Bean Ice Cream, 82
Cupcakes, Espresso, 163–64
Custards
Cappuccino Custard with Cinnamon Cream, 75
Mascarpone Custard with Summer Fruits, 81

D
Dairy products, 24, 182. See also individual foods
Double boilers, 126
Double Chocolate Hot Chocolate, 157

E

Eggs, 25, 182

Equipment, 14–21, 183–84

Espresso Cupcakes with Milk Chocolate Ganache
and White Chocolate Frosting, 163–64

F

Farmers' markets, 182

Fifty-Year Apple Cake, 36

Figs, 37, 125

    Black Mission Fig Honey Cake, 37

    Figamaroles, 119

    Fig Galettes with Cinnamon Marsala Sabayon,
        125–26

Filo, 25, 151

    Apple Filo Napoleons, 63

    Apricot Jalousie Tart, 66

    Bing Cherry Filo Rolls with Cardamom Ice Cream,
        72

    Raspberry Ice Cream Sandwiches, 151–52

Flour, 25

Fondue, Bittersweet Chocolate, 135

French Plum Tart, 107

Frosting, White Chocolate, 163–64

Frozen Lemon Parfait with Lemon Ginger and
Cassis Sauces, 41

Frozen Maple Cream–Pecan Pie, 156

G

Galettes, Fig, with Cinnamon Marsala Sabayon,
125–26

Ganache

    Milk Chocolate Ganache, 163

    Mocha Ganache, 74

Ginger

    Candied Ginger Shortbread Stacks, 77

    Ginger Ice Cream, 180

Glazes

    Chocolate Glaze, 44

    Citrus Glaze, 146–47

Graham Cracker–Banana Cream Napoleons, 134

Grandmother's Apple Cake, 112

Granitas, 85

    Pink Plum Granita with Lime Cookies, 85

    Raspberry Granita, 95

Grape Compote, Concord, 114

H

Hazelnuts

    Hazelnut Sandwich Cookies, 158

    toasting and skinning, 26

    Walnut Hazelnut Bars, 61–62

Honey, 46

    Black Mission Fig Honey Cake, 37

    Honey Cream–Strawberry Parfaits, 46

Honeydew Sorbet, 91–92

Hot Buttered Rum and Banana Compote with
Vanilla Bean Ice Cream, 138

I

Ice baths, 28

Ice cream, 29. *See also Milk shakes*

    Apple Splits, 102

    Cardamom Ice Cream, 180

    Chocolate Chip Ice Cream Cake, 78

    Cinnamon Ice Cream, 180

    Ginger Ice Cream, 180

    Ice Wine Ice Cream, 48

    machines, 17, 20, 179

    Pear–Caramel Swirl Ice Cream, 117–18

    Raspberry Ice Cream, 151

    Raspberry Ice Cream Sandwiches, 151–52

    styles of, 48

    Vanilla Almond Savarin with Ginger Ice Cream
        Balls, 53–54

    Vanilla Bean Ice Cream, 179

Ice Wine Ice Cream with Strawberry Rhubarb
Compote, 48

Indispensable Chocolate Cake, 176–77

Individual German Chocolate Cakes, 108–9

Ingredients

    importance of good-quality, 22

    knowing your, 11

    measuring, 29

    mixing, 29

    sources of, 183–84

L

Ladyfingers, 149–50

Lemons

    Frozen Lemon Parfait with Lemon Ginger and
        Cassis Sauces, 41

    juice, 25

    Lemon Curd, 146–47

    Lemon Mousse with Citrus Compote, 141

    Lemon-Raspberry Bread Pudding, 80

    Meyer Lemon Buttermilk Tart, 160

Limes

    Lime Cookies, 85

    Lime Curd, 55

Local foods, 10

M

Macaroon Pineapple Napoleons, 155

Mango Sauce, 56

Maple Cream–Pecan Pie, Frozen, 156

Marquise, Chestnut Chocolate, 149–50

Mascarpone Custard with Summer Fruits, 81

Measuring, 29

Melon Sorbet Bombe, Three-, 91–92

Meringues

    Brown Sugar Meringues with Strawberries, 38

    Coconut Meringues, 55

Meyer Lemon Buttermilk Tart, 160

Milk, 24

Milk Chocolate Cheesecake, 47

Milk Chocolate Cream, 161

Milk Chocolate Ganache, 163

Milk shakes

    Bourbon Milk Shake, 40

    Chocolate–Peanut Butter Milk Shake, 71

Mocha Ganache, 74

Mousse

    Lemon Mousse with Citrus Compote, 141

    Persimmon Rum Mousse with Crème Fraîche
        and Caramel Sauce, 115

    White Chocolate Coffee Mousse, 44

    White Chocolate Mousse, 86

N

Napoleons, 134

    Apple Filo Napoleons, 63

    Banana Cream–Graham Cracker

        Napoleons, 134

    Macaroon Pineapple Napoleons, 155

    Rice Pudding Napoleon with Rum Raisins, 32–33

Nectarines

    Best-of-Summer Shortcakes, 67

    Mascarpone Custard with Summer Fruits, 81

Nuts. *See also individual nuts*

    Candied Nuts, 180

    tips for, 26

    toasting, 26

O

Oranges, 165

    Chocolate Orange Sabayon, 129–30

    Orange Cream Sauce, 175

    Orange Marmalade Tart, 110

    Orange Pound Cake with Concord Grape

        Compote, 114

    Orange Sherbet, 59

    Rhubarb Orange Tart, 51

    Rum Caramel–Marinated Oranges over

        Vanilla Bean Ice Cream, 165

P

Panna cottas

    Caramel Panna Cotta, 50

    Cinnamon Panna Cotta, 50

    Vanilla Panna Cotta, 50

Papayas, Coconut Pavlovas with Lime Curd,

    Ginger Ice Cream, and, 55

Parfaits

    Frozen Lemon Parfait with Lemon Ginger

        and Cassis Sauces, 41

    Honey Cream–Strawberry Parfaits, 46

Passion Fruit Soufflés with Mango Sauce, 56–57

Pastry Cream, Coconut, 108

Pavlovas, Coconut, with Lime Curd, Ginger

    Ice Cream, and Papayas, 55

Peaches

    Mascarpone Custard with Summer Fruits, 81

    Peach-Blackberry Compote, 77

    Peach Blueberry Trifle, 84

    peeling, 84

    White Peach Melba, 95

Peanuts and peanut butter

    Chocolate–Peanut Butter Milk Shake, 71

    Chocolate–Peanut Butter Truffles, 144

Pears, 117, 182

    Autumn "Summer" Pudding, 99

    Baked Pears with Almond Streusel, 35

    cutting, 29

    Pear–Caramel Swirl Ice Cream with Pecan

        Cookies, 117–18

    sautéing, 111

    Triple-Layer Pear Brioche Sandwiches, 111

Pecans

    Apple Filo Napoleons, 63

    Caramel Pecan Sauce, 108

    Frozen Maple Cream–Pecan Pie, 156

    Individual German Chocolate Cakes, 108–9

    Pecan Cookies, 117–18

    Pecan Crust, 156

    Pumpkin Upside-Down Cake with Cranberry

        Pecan Topping, 120

    toasting, 26

Persimmons

    Persimmon Rum Mousse with Crème Fraîche

        and Caramel Sauce, 115

    puree, 115

    ripening Hachiya, 115

Pies

    Frozen Maple Cream–Pecan Pie, 156

    Pie Dough, 171

    prebaked crust for, 171

    Raspberry Pie, 89

Pineapple

    cutting, 155

    Macaroon Pineapple Napoleons, 155

Pink Plum Granita with Lime Cookies, 85

Pistachios, 182

Plums, 107

    French Plum Tart, 107

Pink Plum Granita with Lime Cookies, 85

Poppy Seed Cake, 69

Potlucks, 61

Puddings

    Apple Caramel Bread Pudding, 137

    Autumn "Summer" Pudding, 99

    Lemon-Raspberry Bread Pudding, 80

    Rice Pudding Napoleon with Rum Raisins, 32–33

Puff pastry

    Blitz Puff Pastry, 168

    French Plum Tart, 107

    Rice Pudding Napoleon with Rum Raisins,

        32–33

Pumpkin, 120

    Pumpkin Cake, 122–23

    Pumpkin Upside-Down Cake with Cranberry

        Pecan Topping, 120

    Pumpkin Zuccotto, 122–23

Q

Quince, Baked, Walnut Shortcakes with, 131

R

Raisins

    Fifty-Year Apple Cake, 36

    Ricotta Cheesecake with Dried Cherries and

        Golden Raisins, 127

    Rum Raisins, 32

Raspberries, 89, 101, 151

    Berry Crème Fraîche Cake, 69–70

    Lemon-Raspberry Bread Pudding, 80

    Raspberry Granita, 95

    Raspberry–Honey Cream Tartlets, 101

    Raspberry Ice Cream, 151

    Raspberry Ice Cream Sandwiches, 151–52

    Raspberry Pie, 89

    Raspberry Sauce, 174

    Red Berry–White Chocolate Trifles, 86–88

    White Peach Melba, 95

Red Berry–White Chocolate Trifles, 86–88

Rhubarb, 51

Rhubarb Orange Tart, 51

Strawberry Rhubarb Compote, 48

Rice Pudding Napoleon with Rum Raisins, 32–33

Ricotta Cheesecake with Dried Cherries and Golden Raisins, 127

Rum
Hot Buttered Rum and Banana Compote, 138
Persimmon Rum Mousse, 115
Rum Caramel–Marinated Oranges, 165
Rum Raisins, 32

Rustic Blueberry Tart, 93

S

Sabayons
Chocolate Orange Sabayon, 129–30
Cinnamon Marsala Sabayon, 125–26
whisking, 126

Sauces
Berry Sauce, 86
Blueberry Sauce, 82
Caramel Pecan Sauce, 108
Caramel Sauce, 173
Cassis Sauce, 41
Chocolate Sauce, 173
Lemon Ginger Sauce, 41
Mango Sauce, 56
Orange Cream Sauce, 175
Raspberry Sauce, 174
White Chocolate Sauce, 139

Savarin, Vanilla Almond, 53–54

Seasons, eating with, 10, 30, 64, 96, 132

Sherbet, Orange, 59

Shortbread Stacks, Candied Ginger, with Peach-Blackberry Compote, 77

Shortcakes
Best-of-Summer Shortcakes, 67
Walnut Shortcakes with Baked Quince, 131

Sodas, Strawberry Ginger, with Orange Sherbet, 59

Sorbet
Cantaloupe Sorbet, 91
Honeydew Sorbet, 91–92
Three-Melon Sorbet Bombe, 91–92
vodka in, 92
Watermelon Sorbet, 91–92

Soufflés, Passion Fruit, with Mango Sauce, 56–57

Spices, 26

Storage tips, 29

Strawberries, 28–29, 38, 182
Brown Sugar Meringues with Strawberries, 38
Honey Cream–Strawberry Parfaits, 46
Red Berry–White Chocolate Trifles, 86–88
Strawberry Ginger Sodas with Orange Sherbet, 59
Strawberry Rhubarb Compote, 48

Sugar, 26–27
Sugar Syrup, 91
vanilla, 54

T

Tarts
Apricot Jalousie Tart, 66
Caramel Chocolate-Chunk Tart, 43
French Plum Tart, 107
Meyer Lemon Buttermilk Tart, 160
Orange Marmalade Tart, 110
prebaked crust for, 171
Raspberry–Honey Cream Tartlets, 101
Rhubarb Orange Tart, 51
Rustic Blueberry Tart, 93
Tart Dough, 170

Three-Melon Sorbet Bombe, 91–92

Timing, 28

Trifles, 84, 161
Peach Blueberry Trifle, 84
Red Berry–White Chocolate Trifles, 86–88
Trifle Cake, 178
Triple Chocolate Trifles, 161

Triple-Layer Pear Brioche Sandwiches, 111

Truffles
Chocolate Mocha Truffles, 143
Chocolate–Peanut Butter Truffles, 144
scooping, 143

V

Vanilla, 27, 53, 182
sugar, 54
Vanilla Almond Savarin with Ginger Ice Cream Balls, 53–54
Vanilla Bean Ice Cream, 179
Vanilla Crème Anglaise, 175
Vanilla Panna Cotta, 50

W

Walnuts
Fifty-Year Apple Cake, 36
toasting, 26
Walnut Cake with Chocolate Orange Sabayon and Vanilla Crème Anglaise, 129–30
Walnut Hazelnut Bars, 61–62
Walnut Shortcakes with Baked Quince, 131

Watermelon Sorbet, 91–92

White chocolate
Double Chocolate Hot Chocolate, 157
Honey Cream–Strawberry Parfaits, 46
Red Berry–White Chocolate Trifles, 86–88
Triple Chocolate Trifles, 161
White Chocolate Coffee Mousse, 44
White Chocolate Cream, 161
White Chocolate Frosting, 163–64
White Chocolate Mousse, 86
White Chocolate Sauce, 139

White Peach Melba, 95

Wine Ice Cream, Ice, 48

Z

Zuccotto, Pumpkin, 122–23

table of equivalents

THE EXACT EQUIVALENTS IN THE FOLLOWING TABLES HAVE BEEN ROUNDED FOR CONVENIENCE.

LIQUID/DRY MEASURES

U.S.	METRIC
1/4 teaspoon	1.25 milliliters
1/2 teaspoon	2.5 milliliters
1 teaspoon	5 milliliters
1 tablespoon (3 teaspoons)	15 milliliters
1 fluid ounce (2 tablespoons)	30 milliliters
1/4 cup	60 milliliters
1/3 cup	80 milliliters
1/2 cup	120 milliliters
1 cup	240 milliliters
1 pint (2 cups)	480 milliliters
1 quart (4 cups, 32 ounces)	960 milliliters
1 gallon (4 quarts)	3.84 liters
1 ounce (by weight)	28 grams
1 pound	454 grams
2.2 pounds	1 kilogram

LENGTH

U.S.	METRIC
1/8 inch	3 millimeters
1/4 inch	6 millimeters
1/2 inch	12 millimeters
1 inch	2.5 centimeters

OVEN TEMPERATURE

FAHRENHEIT	CELSIUS	GAS
250	120	1/2
275	140	1
300	150	2
325	160	3
350	180	4
375	190	5
400	200	6
425	220	7
450	230	8
475	240	9
500	260	10